THE REFERENCE SHELF   VOLUME 36 NUMBER 6

CIVIL RIGHTS

EDITED BY
GRANT S. McCLELLAN

Associate Editor, Current Magazine

THE H. W. WILSON COMPANY
NEW YORK   1964

THE REFERENCE SHELF

The books in this series reprint articles, excerpts from books, and addresses on current issues, social trends, and other aspects of American life, and occasional surveys of foreign countries. There are six separately bound numbers in each volume, all of which are generally published in the same calendar year. One number is a collection of recent speeches on a variety of subjects; each of the remaining numbers is devoted to a single subject and gives background information and discussion from varying points of view, followed by a comprehensive bibliography.

Subscribers to the current volume receive the books as issued. The subscription rate is $12 ($15 foreign) for a volume of six numbers. The price of single numbers is $3 each.

23409

PREFACE

In the future the mid-twentieth century may well rank as one of the politically creative eras in America's history, a period in which Negro demands for equality contributed to the enlargement of individual freedoms for American citizens, both black and white. For it is clear that the present concern about civil rights is largely due to the Negro's militant demand to enter into the mainstream of American life, and to be treated on exactly the same basis as any other citizen.

The traditional freedoms—freedom of speech and association, as well as others—have been reinforced and enlarged in this period. New freedoms are envisaged as necessary in a world that otherwise seems to close in on the individual in terms of both a more complex society, economically and socially, and a world under danger of sudden nuclear extinction.

There is also a growing interest in the protection of human rights throughout the world. Despite its dedication to individual liberties on a universal basis, the United States has hitherto not been greatly concerned with the extension of civil rights much beyond its own borders. This interest is only now arising as a matter of United States policy in its relations with other countries.

The following compilation surveys the Negroes' demands for advances in recognition of their civil rights in American society. It also considers the recent advances made in the protection of traditional civil rights, the claims for the extension of rights into new areas, and the efforts toward achievement of human rights on a global basis.

The editor wishes to thank both the authors and the publishers for permission to reprint the selections included in this volume.

GRANT S. McCLELLAN

December 1964

CONTENTS

I. THE MID-CENTURY
CIVIL RIGHTS MOVEMENT

EDITOR'S INTRODUCTION

One of the outstanding leaders of the contemporary Negro civil rights movement, the Reverend Martin Luther King, Jr., has said that three simple words can describe the nature of the social revolution now taking place and what Negroes really want. They are the words "all," "now," and "here."

The excerpts included in this section bear out Dr. King's view in many ways. Two articles review the ten years which have passed since the Supreme Court's landmark decision banning segregation in the public schools. The first article notes the growth and progress of the civil rights movement since the 1954 decision; the second discusses the increasingly wide role the Supreme Court has played in upholding and extending civil rights.

Next, various leaders of the civil rights movement present their views. Martin Luther King, Jr., founder and president of the Southern Christian Leadership Conference, leader of the nonviolent movement in the South, and winner of the 1964 Nobel Prize for Peace, speaks to the theme "Why We Can't Wait." The National Urban League suggests that a massive aid plan is necessary for the Negro, one comparable with the Marshall Plan, undertaken by the United States to help restore the economy of postwar Europe. In the following selection, five Negro leaders set forth their goals in such areas as education, employment, housing, and social acceptance; they then present some ideas as to how those goals may be achieved. The five men interviewed are Roy Wilkins, executive secretary of the National Association for the Advancement of Colored People (NAACP); James Farmer, national director of the Congress of Racial Equality (CORE); Bayard Rustin, "architect" of the 1963 March on Washington; Adam Clayton Powell, minister and Representative (Democrat) from New York; and the Reverend Milton Galamison, New York minister and school boycott leader.

In the closing selections, two educators offer possible solutions to two of the Negroes' greatest problems. In discussing equality in education, John H. Fisher, president of Columbia University's Teachers College, points out that the average Negro child, because of his socioeconomic background, comes to shcool with a built-in handicap. He suggests that since our educational system already gives special attention to children with mental and physical handicaps, perhaps it could also provide "compensatory opportunity" for those put at a disadvantage by racial prejudice or poor home environment.

Following this, Eli Ginzberg, an economist, states his view that equality of educational opportunity must be matched with equality in employment and opportunity for economic gain. He points out that as regards unemployment and the obsolescence of unskilled labor the Negro is in the same position as the economically depressed white. He suggests, therefore, that the necessary legislation be enacted to open up the labor market and thus provide Negroes and whites with an equal opportunity for economic improvement.

SINCE THE SUPREME COURT SPOKE [1]

Shortly after noon on May 17, 1954, reporters waiting in the Supreme Court press room for what they thought would be routine opinions were suddenly told to go to the courtroom. There Chief Justice Earl Warren was reading his opinion for the Court in Case No. 1 on the docket that term, *Brown et al. v. Board of Education of Topeka et al.* For minutes the audience listened without a sure clue to the outcome. Then the Chief Justice read:

> We come then to the question presented. Does segregation of children in public schools solely on the basis of race, even though the physical facilities and other "tangible" factors may be equal, deprive the children of the minority group of equal educational opportunities? We believe that it does.

Ten years after that moment in history we can see it as the spark of a revolution in American attitudes toward the race problem. During the turbulent decade the stereotype of the apathetic,

[1] From article by Anthony Lewis, member, Washington bureau, New York *Times*. New York *Times Magazine*. p 9+. My. 10, '64. © 1964 by The New York Times Company. Reprinted by permission.

satisfied Negro has forever been destroyed; the Federal Government has abandoned a hands-off attitude of eighty years' standing and come to the point of total commitment against racial segregation; the hypocrisy of the South and the complacency of the North have been undermined by the new Negro militancy. Perhaps most important, the indifference of white America toward the race problem has been shattered; everyone knows that it is the great domestic issue facing this country and will be in the years ahead. . . .

Change of the dimensions experienced in the racial field over the last decade does not just begin at a point in time; it builds on history. There were pressures working for change in American race relations before 1954: the industrialization and urbanization of the South, bringing with them social anonymity; the weakening of regional differences in this country by the impact of mass communications; universal training in armed forces that were being desegregated; a slow growth in the Negro's legal and political power.

But revolutions require a spark. For the revolution in this country's racial situation, it was surely the school decision. . . .

The Lessons of the Decision

What, then, have been the results and the lessons of that Supreme Court decision of ten years ago. . . ?

It may, more than anything else, have given the Negro hope. The Supreme Court of the United States, pinnacle of the white Establishment, had understood at last that segregated institutions were not and could not be equal. The law was on the Negro's side now—often a faraway law, it is true, offering little immediate protection against the local pressures of white supremacy, but still giving hope of ultimate justice.

It gave the Negro a courage and a will that few, or even he himself, had known he had. Who will forget the picture of a few little colored children walking into a school past jeering, hating white faces? After that, the children had to endure in many cases a life without friends in school, often a life of secret abuse and terror. Their parents faced economic reprisal as well as fear for the children. And still they persisted.

The struggle to carry out the school decision encouraged Negroes to speak out for other rights. It surely helped to inspire such events of this remarkable decade as the Montgomery bus boycott, the Freedom Rides, the sit-ins. Even in the voting field, the school struggle was relevant. Many outsiders believed it would be more logical for Negroes in the South to concentrate first on obtaining the right to vote. But that right, basic as it was, may have been too impersonal to arouse the Southern Negro from apathy and fear. It took the drama of school desegregation and then of the protest movements to bring the possibility of freedom alive; then the Negroes began standing in those long, patient lines outside registrars' offices.

Violent Southern resistance to the school decision awakened Northern white opinion to the meaning of racism. Most Northerners had gone through life without thinking about how it would feel to have a black skin. Then came those scenes outside the schools in Little Rock and New Orleans—the women screaming "Nigger," the mob clawing at a Catholic priest. Those in the North who saw those events on television, or read about them, were not likely to miss the unreasoning hatred and inhumanity. The North is not pure of heart, but its official institutions work to eradicate inequality, not to maintain it.

The Federal Government was as last moved to action in race matters. President Eisenhower, who had done nothing to encourage acceptance of the Supreme Court decision, and was planning to do nothing, intervened when Governor Orval Faubus [Democrat, Arkansas] and his mob at Little Rock forced the Federal hand.

Southern excesses in other areas similarly aroused Northern opinion and the Federal Government. Brutal assaults on the Freedom Riders in Alabama in 1961 led Attorney General Robert F. Kennedy to dispatch a force of marshals and then to ask the Interstate Commerce Commission for an order that has virtually wiped out segregation in bus and rail terminals. The pictures of dogs assaulting Negro demonstrators in Birmingham in 1963 were instrumental in President Kennedy's decision to propose the broadest civil rights legislation ever seriously urged on Congress.

These years have demonstrated the extraordinary role of law as a shaper of opinion in this country. Events proved the foolishness of President Eisenhower's view that the law could not affect racial prejudice. "I don't believe you can change the hearts of men with laws or decisions" was what he often said.

That was just what the Supreme Court had written in 1896, in the decision upholding the constitutionality of separate facilities for Negroes. "Legislation is powerless," the opinion said, "to eradicate racial instincts or to abolish distinctions based upon physical differences."

The point is not that laws and decisions can end all racial feelings; of course not. But they can either encourage or inhibit prejudice. As a wiser Supreme Court said in 1950, when it held that a Negro university student could not be made to sit at a segregated desk:

The removal of the state restrictions will not necessarily abate the individual and group predilections, prejudices and choices. But at the very least the state will not be depriving appellant of the opportunity to secure acceptance by his fellow students on his own merit.

Moreover, law does affect patterns of external conduct, slowly forcing people to conform at least superficially to new standards. Over time, habits may affect feelings. . . .

Now, at last this country's deep underlying reverence for law seems to be prevailing in most of the South. The South has begun to learn that the Supreme Court's interpretation of the Constitution, when it has the support of the rest of the country, cannot be resisted indefinitely. It has begun to learn that change is inevitable in race relations, that the movement for equal rights has powerful momentum behind it. It has begun to learn that the South cannot stand alone, that it is part of a larger country and that the United States is part of a world in which men with white skins are outnumbered by the black and brown and yellow.

But a companion lesson is that law is not enough. This is a moralistic as well as a legalistic country, and the pace of change in race relations was as revolutionary as it was because the American conscience was touched.

Dr. Martin Luther King Jr., and his doctrine of nonviolent resistance, one of the remarkable developments of the period, combined the American religious tradition with the spirit of Gandhian protest. The young followers of Dr. King, sitting quietly at lunch counters as they were verbally and physically abused, brought a needed spiritual content to the movement for racial justice.

Those brave students ended, moreover, the possibility of anyone taking seriously the South's traditional claim that *its* Negroes were contented—outside agitators were causing all the trouble. The peaceful protesters caught the imagination and sympathy of the North.

Looking to the Future

Now, as we stand at the start of a new phase in race relations, the Negro sees much that is undone. He knows that he is twice as likely to be unemployed as a white man, that his median family income is only half the white family's. In the rural counties of the South recognition of Negro rights is still miniscule, and there is intransigence in Southern cities from Birmingham to Jackson. United States senators will stand up and admit men are kept from voting because of their color. In Mississippi it is still worth a Negro's job—and perhaps his life—to try to vote.

In practical terms not much of a dent has been made on school segregation; throughout the South only 1 per cent of Negro children are actually in classes with whites. In the great cities—North and South—it is Negroes who more and more fill up the slums and attend the worst schools. In innumerable ways a colored skin remains an enormous handicap in the United States.

The white man sees the problem from the opposite end of the telescope. He sees what has happened in ten years and thinks it is astonishingly much. Segregation has ended at hundreds of lunch counters and hotels and theaters in the South and has all but disappeared in transportation. Every Southern state but Mississippi has made at least a token start on school desegragation. [Three months after the publication of this article, in August 1964, seventeen Negro first graders were quietly admitted to four previously all-white schools in Biloxi, Mississippi.—Ed.] Negro political power has risen, South and North. The Supreme Court has removed the legal basis for virtually every official discrimination on account of race.

For the first time a President—Kennedy, then Johnson [see speeches, "A Moral Issue" and "An Act of Lawmaking," Section II, below]—has condemned segregation as morally unjust. Congress, after eighty years of silence, has passed . . . [three] civil rights acts . . . that bring Federal power to bear in many new ways.

As we look ahead, it is possible to foresee a gradual end to the remaining official discrimination in the South. The force of the effort to open the polling places and the schools and the parks will mount. One can even hope, within the next ten years, to see some senators from the Deep South liberated from the awful weight of racist politics.

Not that the South can be forgotten now. It will take the most grueling effort by the Justice Department—and perhaps more legislaion—to end the blatant discrimination that remains there.

But it is as a national problem that race relations will primarily be seen in the next decade. The challenge is to overcome the legacy of inequality everywhere—to open unions and companies to Negro workers, to provide education and training that Negroes have not had, to let Negroes escape from the slums, to break the cycle of poverty and ignorance. After the cruel refusal of white plumbers to work by the side of a few Negroes and Puerto Ricans in New York City we know that not only the South has a race problem. . . .

In a sense it should not be disturbing that all the country is now engaged in the race problem. The pretense that the problem existed only in the South was just that, a pretense, and it is better to have the truth out, however painful it is.

Indeed, one of the greatest changes in the last ten years has been simply an awareness of the racial issue. It is hard to recall the pervasive indifference to racial discrimination in this country ten years ago, or even more recently. We have come a long way when thousands of Northern college students sign on to spend their summers helping Negroes to register in the South or to get a better education in the North.

In his *An American Dilemma,* published in 1944, Gunnar Myrdal [Swedish economist] wrote:

The Negro problem is not only America's greatest failure but also America's great opportunity for the future. If America should follow its own deepest convictions, its well-being at home would be increased directly. At the same time America's prestige and power abroad would rise. . . . America can demonstrate that justice, equality and cooperation are possible between white and colored people. . . . *America is free to choose whether the Negro shall remain her liability or become her opportunity.*

CHANGES ON A BROAD FRONT [2]

This past decade—which may eventually stand alone as an era of legal history—began on that May day in 1954 when the Court ruled that the assignment of students by race to public schools was unconstitutional. . . .

[With that decision in *Brown et al. v. Board of Education of Topeka et al.,* the Supreme Court] became a major participant in the social life of the nation. It broke a deadlock that had stymied American government for years and it pointed down the road of equality, a road that, with the passage of the Civil Rights Bill, one can say most American have now chosen to walk.

This past year, the Court similarly became a major participant in political life when it ruled that the seats in both houses of state legislatures must be apportioned among citizens according to population. Again, the Court broke a deadlock that had stalled the processes of government and pointed down another road to equality. From the initial reaction to that decision, one can suspect that most Americans will also be willing to walk that way.

In both instances, the Court was demonstrating its new role in government. This is a role of active participation in the creative activity that keeps government apace of public needs. Traditionally, the Court has been a brake on innovation rather than a force for change, but in the areas of discrimination and apportionment it became the moving force in a government that was otherwise motionless.

In this new role, the Court has moved quickly and aggressively to compel changes in American government when the existing situation did not square absolutely with the Court's view of the Constitution. It has not hesitated to hold acts of Congress or of state legislatures unconstitutional or to declare substantial changes in constitutional interpretations. . . .

In 1945, the direction the Court would take in the future was not at all clear. It had survived, just barely, from the conflicts

[2] From "1954-64 Truly an Era," by James E. Clayton, staff reporter, Washington *Post.* Washington *Post.* p E1+. Je. 28, '64. Reprinted by permission.

over New Deal legislation and the justices were sorely divided as to what their role in government should be. It was not until the mid-1950's that the new era began.

This era came into being, ironically enough, when the rest of government reversed its general philosophy that had led to the Court fight of the 1930's. In the early Depression years, the Court had blocked the efforts of a creative Congress and a creative Executive to change the status quo in economic life.

In the 1950's, both the Federal Government and the states refused to meet similar demands to change the status quo in other areas. States did not respond when urban and suburban voters complained that they were underrepresented in state governments and when enlightened lawyers called for modernization of the criminal law. The Federal Government did not respond to calls for change in the area of civil rights.

These demands for action coincided with the rising dominance on the Court of the school of thought which holds that the justices should play an active role in public life. Thus, the results that followed were natural; power abhors a vacuum and the Court stepped in to fill the void.

Whether this era is approaching its end remains to be seen. It could end through a rebuke delivered from outside the court, such as the constitutional amendments that were proposed last year to undermine its power. Or it could end of its own force. There is now some evidence that the latter is becoming true; that the Court has turned its constitutional corner and is about to pause for a while to regroup. . . .

If this is the point at which the court pauses for a moment, it is a remarkably fitting point because of the great amount of decisive action in so many areas of the law during the last two terms. . . .

Civil Rights for Others

The great area of the Court's work this year . . . was in apportionment. It held six to three, that congressional districts and houses of all state legislatures must be apportioned according to population. . . .

In two other areas of law, the Court indicated it is now facing a direction quite different from the position it occupied ten years ago. It is quickly forcing higher standards of criminal law upon the states and it is treating individual rights with a new tenderness.

What the Court is doing to criminal law can be described in two ways. One is to say it is nationalizing the law by forcing the states to become like each other and like the Federal Government. The other is to say it is strengthening the guarantees of individual liberties.

Regardless of which way the process is described, there is a clear majority on the Court for it. In some instances, as when the states were required in 1963 to provide attorneys for all poor persons charged wih crime, all the Justices agreed. In others, as when the Fifth Amendment's self-incrimination clause was made binding on the states, the vote is closer; in this case it was five to two. The real division among Court members comes not on the idea that standards of justice be raised but under what constitutional standard this should be done and what details should be changed. . . .

In the related area of civil liberties—passports, loyalty oaths, citizenship—the attitude of the Court's majority, if not its specific action, is new.

The Court held unconstitutional two Washington state loyalty oaths this year by a vote of seven to two. It held unconstitutional a provision taking citizenship away from naturalized Americans who return to their homeland for three years by a vote of five to three. It voided a law saying the use of a passport by anyone required to register under the Subversive Activities Control Act was a crime. . . .

These are cases that might well have been decided differently ten years ago. . . . There has been much talk that the Court has been merely amending the Constitution to conform with the whims of its majority. It is said to be doing so in all four of the areas mentioned above.

But this kind of comment misses the mark. Every student of the Court knows that major decisions are almost always interpretations of the Constitution's vague phrases. And every interpretation of these phrases is always regarded as an amendment of the phrases by those who disagree with the interpretation. The real fight in the Court during the last twenty years has been over whether and when the justices should use their power of interpretation—not over the issue of whether they are wrongfully using their power to amend the Constitution.

This is what the fight over the Court's role in government is all about. To Justice [John Marshall] Harlan, the spokesman for those who believe in judicial restraint, the Court must defer heavily to the views of other branches of government on what is constitutional. To Justice [Hugo L.] Black, the proponent of judicial activism, the Court is obligated to defer to no one and to express its views even if it means the Court becomes the leading branch of the government. It is clear now that Black has won this fight; what remains is the direction in which the victory leads the Court.

"WHY WE CAN'T WAIT" [3]

People . . . say today: "What more will the Negro expect if he gains such rights as integrated schools, public facilities, voting rights and progress in housing? Will he, like Oliver Twist, demand more?" What is implied is the amazing assumption that society has the right to bargain with the Negro for the freedom which inherently belongs to him. . . .

The relevant question is not: "What more does the Negro want?" but rather: "How can we make freedom real and substantial for our colored citizens? What just course will ensure the greatest speed and completeness? And how do we combat opposition and overcome obstacles arising from the defaults of the past?"

New ways are needed to handle the issue because we have come to a new stage in the development of our nation and of one in ten of its people. The surging power of the Negro revolt and the genuineness of good will that has come from many white Americans indicate that the time is ripe for broader thinking and action.

The Negro today is not struggling for some abstract, vague rights, but for concrete and prompt improvement in his way of life. What will it profit him to be able to send his children to

[3] From "The Days to Come," Chapter 8 of *Why We Can't Wait*, by the Reverend Martin Luther King, Jr., founder and president of the Southern Christian Leadership Conference. Harper and Row. New York. '63. p 139-69. Copyright © 1964 by Martin Luther King, Jr. Reprinted with the permission of Harper and Row, Publishers. (An adaptation of this chapter appeared in *Life*. 56:98-112. My. 15, '64.)

an integrated school if the family income is insufficient to buy them school clothes? What will he gain by being permitted to move to an integrated neighborhood if he cannot afford to do so because he is unemployed or has a low-paying job with no future? . . . Of what advantage is it to the Negro to establish that he can be served in integrated restaurants, or accommodated in integrated hotels, if he is bound to the kind of financial servitude which will not allow him to take a vacation or even to take his wife out to dine? Negroes must not only have the right to go into any establishment open to the public but they must also be absorbed into our economic system in such a manner that they can afford to exercise that right.

The struggle for rights is, at bottom, a struggle for opportunities. In asking for something special, the Negro is not seeking charity. He does not want to languish on welfare rolls any more than the next man. He does not want to be given a job he cannot handle. Neither, however, does he want to be told that there is no place where he can be trained to handle it. So, with equal opportunity must come the practical, realistic aid which will equip him to seize it. Giving a pair of shoes to a man who has not learned to walk is a cruel jest.

Special measures for the deprived have always been accepted in principle by the United States. The National Urban League, in an excellent statement [see "A 'Marshall Plan' for the American Negro," this section, below] has underlined the fact that we find nothing strange about Marshall Plan and technical assistance to handicapped peoples around the world, and suggested that we can do no less for our own handicapped multitudes. Throughout history, we have adhered to this principle. It was the principle behind land grants to farmers who fought in the Revolutionary Army. It was inherent in the establishment of child labor laws, social security, unemployment compensation, manpower retraining programs and countless other measures that the nation accepted as logical and moral.

During World War II, our fighting men were deprived of certain advantages and opportunities. To make up for this, they were given a package of veterans' rights, significantly called a "Bill of Rights." The major features of this GI Bill of Rights included subsidies for trade school or college education, with living expenses provided during the period of study. Veterans were given special concessions enabling them to buy homes without cash, with lower interest rates and easier repayment terms. They could negotiate loans from banks to launch businesses, using the Government as an endorser of any losses. They received special points to place them ahead in competition for civil service jobs. They were provided with medical care and long-term financial grants if their physical condition had been impaired by their military service. In addition to these legally granted rights, a strong social climate for many years favored the preferential employment of veterans in all walks of life.

In this way, the nation was compensating the veteran for his time lost, in school or in his career or in business. Such compensatory treatment was approved by the majority of Americans. Certainly the Negro has been deprived. Few people consider the fact that, in addition to being enslaved for two centuries, the Negro was, during all those years, robbed of the wages of his toil. No amount of gold could provide an adequate compensation for the exploitation and humiliation of the Negro in America down through the centuries. Not all the wealth of this affluent society could meet the bill. Yet a price can be placed on unpaid wages. The ancient common law has always provided a remedy for the appropriation of the labor of one human being by another. This law should be made to apply for American Negroes. The payment should be in the form of a massive program by the Government of special, compensatory measures which could be regarded as a settlement in accordance with the accepted practice of common law. Such measures would certainly be less expensive than any computation based on two centuries of unpaid wages and accumulated interest.

A Bill of Rights for the Disadvantaged

I am proposing, therefore, that, just as we granted a GI Bill of Rights to war veterans, America launch a broad-based and gigantic Bill of Rights for the Disadvantaged, our veterans of the long siege of denial.

Such a bill could adapt almost every concession given to the returning soldier without imposing an undue burden on our economy. A Bill of Rights for the Disadvantaged would immediately transform the conditions of Negro life. The most profound alteration would not reside so much in the specific grants as in the basic psychological and motivational transformation of the Negro. I would challenge skeptics to give such a bold new approach a test for the next decade. I contend that the decline in school dropouts, family breakups, crime rates, illegitimacy, swollen relief rolls and other social evils would stagger the imagination. Change in human psychology is normally a slow process, but it is safe to predict that, when a people is ready for change as the Negro has shown himself ready today, the response is bound to be rapid and constructive.

Negroes and Poor Whites

While Negroes form the vast majority of America's disadvantaged, there are millions of white poor who would also benefit from such a bill. The moral justification for special measures for Negroes is rooted in the robberies inherent in the institution of slavery. Many poor whites, however, were the derivative victims of slavery. As long as labor was cheapened by the involuntary servitude of the black man, the freedom of white labor, especially in the South, was little more than a myth. It was free only to bargain from the depressed base imposed by slavery upon the whole labor market. Nor did this derivative bondage end when formal slavery gave way to the *de facto* slavery of discrimination and the humiliation of poverty if not of color. They are chained by the weight of discrimination, though its badge of degradation does not mark them. It corrupts their lives, frustrates their opportunities and withers their education. In one sense it is more evil for them, because it has confused so many by prejudice that they have supported their own oppressors.

It is a simple matter of justice that America, in dealing creatively with the task of raising the Negro from backwardness, should also be rescuing a large stratum of the forgotten white poor. A Bill of Rights for the Disadvantaged could mark the rise of a new era, in which the full resources of the society would be used to attack the tenacious poverty which so paradoxically exists in the midst of plenty.

The nation will also have to find the answer to full employment, including a more imaginative approach than has yet been conceived for neutralizing the perils of automation. . . . The energetic and creative expansion of work opportunities, in both the public and private sectors of our economy, is an imperative worthy of the richest nation on earth, whose abundance is an embarrassment as long as millions of poor are imprisoned and constantly self-renewed within an expanding population.

In addition to such an economic program, a social-work apparatus on a large scale is required. Whole generations have been left behind as the majority of the population advanced. These lost generations have never learned basic social skills on a functional level—the skills of reading, writing, arithmetic; of applying for jobs; of exercising the rights of citizenship, including the right to vote. Moreover, rural and urban poverty has not only stultified lives; it has created emotional disturbances, many of which find expression in antisocial acts. The most tragic victims are children whose impoverished parents, frantically struggling day by day for food and a place to live, have been unable to create the stable home necessary for the wholesome growth of young minds.

Opportunities and the means to exploit them are, however, still inadequate to assure equality, justice and decency in our national life. There is an imperative need also for legislation to outlaw our present grotesque legal mores. We find ourselves in a society where the supreme law of the land, the Constitution, is rendered inoperative in vast areas of the nation. State, municipal, county laws and practices negate constitutional mandates as blatantly as if each community were an independent medieval duchy. Even though strong civil rights legislation is written into the books and even if a Bill of Rights for the Disadvantaged were to follow, enforcement will still meet with massive resistance in many parts of the country. . . .

The pattern of future action must be examined not only from the standpoint of the strengths inherent in the civil rights movement, but simultaneously from a study of the resistance we have yet to face. While we can celebrate that the civil rights movement has come of age, we must also recognize that the basic recalcitrance of the South has not yet been broken. True, substantial progress has been made: it is deeply significant that a powerful financial and industrial force has emerged in some Southern regions, which is prepared to tolerate change in order to avoid costly chaos. This group in turn permits the surfacing of middle-class elements who are further splitting the monolithic front of segregation. Southern church, labor and human relations groups today articulate sentiments that only yesterday would have been pronounced treasonable in the region. Nevertheless, a deeply entrenched social force, convinced that it need yield nothing of substantial importance, continues to dominate Southern life. And even in the North, the will to preserve the status quo maintains a rock-like hardness underneath the cosmetic surface.

Working with Others

In order to assure that the work of democracy so well begun in the summer of 1963 will move forward steadily in the seasons to come, the Negro freedom movement will need to secure and extend its alliances with like-minded groups in the larger community. . . .

In the case of organized labor, an alliance with the Negro civil rights movement is not a matter of choice but a necessity. If Negroes have almost no rights in the South, labor has few more; if Negroes have inadequate political influence in Congress, labor is barely better off; if automation is a threat to Negroes, it is equally a menace to organized labor. . . .

Another necessary alliance is with the Federal Government. It is the obligation of Government to move resolutely to the side of the freedom movement. There is a right and a wrong side in this conflict and the Government does not belong in the middle.

Without the resources of the Federal Government the task of achieving practical civil rights must overwhelm voluntary organization. It is not generally realized that the burden of court decisions, such as the Supreme Court decision on school desegregation, places the responsibility on the individual Negro who is compelled to bring a suit in order to obtain his rights. In effect, the most impoverished Americans, facing powerfully equipped adversaries, are required to finance and conduct complex litigation that may involve tens of thousands of dollars. To have shaped remedies in this form for existing inequities in our national life was in itself a concession to segregationists. A solution can be achieved only if the government assumes the responsibility for all legal proceedings, facing the reality that the poor and the unemployed already fight an unequal daily struggle to stay alive. To be forced to accumulate resources for legal actions imposes intolerable hardships on the already overburdened. . . .

[Now] a new stage in the civil rights has been reached, which calls for a new policy. What has changed is our strength. The upsurge of power in the civil rights movement has given it greater maneuverability and substantial security. It is now strong enough to form alliances, to make commitments in exchange for pledges and, if the pledges are unredeemed, it remains powerful enough to walk out without being shattered or weakened.

Negroes have traditionally positioned themseves too far from the inner arena of political decision. Few other minority groups have maintained a political aloofness and a nonpartisan posture as rigidly and as long as have Negroes. The Germans, Irish, Italians and Jews, after a period of acclimatization, moved inside political formations and exercised influence. Negroes, partly by choice but substantially by exclusion, have operated outside of the political structures, functioning instead essentially as a pressure group with limited effect.

For some time this reticence protected the Negro from corruption and manipulation by political bosses. The cynical district leader directing his ignorant flock to vote blindly at his dictation is a relatively rare phenomenon in Negro life. The very few Negro political bosses have no gullible following. Those who give them support do so because they are persuaded that these men are their only available forthright spokesmen. By and large, Negroes remain essentially skeptical, issue-oriented and independent-minded. Their lack of formal learning is no barrier when it comes to making intelligent choices among alternatives.

The Negroes' real problem has been that they have seldom had adequate choices. Political life, as a rule, did not attract the best elements of the Negro community, and white candidates who represented their views were few and far between. However, in avoiding the trap of domination by unworthy leaders, Negroes fell into the bog of political inactivity. They avoided victimization by any political group by withholding a significant commitment to any organization or individual.

The price they paid was reflected in the meager influence they could exercise for a positive program. But in the more recent years, as a result of their direct-action programs, their political potentiality has become manifest both to themselves and to the political leadership. An active rethinking is taking place in all Negro circles concerning their role in political life. The conclusion is already certain: it is time for Negroes to abandon abstract political neutrality and become less timid about voting alliances. If we bear in mind that alliance does not mean reliance, our independence will remain inviolate. We can and should selectively back candidates whose records justify confidence. We can, because of our strength; we should, because those who work with us must feel we can help them concretely. Conversely, those who deny us their support should not feel that no one will get our help, but instead they must understand that, when they spurn us, it is likely not only that they will lose but that their opponent will gain.

The Negro potential for political power is now substantial. Negroes are strategically situated in large cities, especially in the North but also in the South, and these cities in turn are decisive in state elections. These same states are the key in a presidential race and frequently determine the nomination. This unique factor gives Negroes enormous leverage in the balance of power. The effects of this leverage are already evident. In South Carolina, for example, the ten-thousand-vote margin that gave President Kennedy his victory in 1960 was the Negro vote. Since then some half a million new Negro voters have been added to Southern registration rolls. Today a shift in the Negro vote could upset the outcome of several state contests and affect the result of a presidential election.

Moreover, the subjective elements of political power—persistence, aggressiveness and discipline—are also attributes of the new movement. Political leaders are infinitely respectful toward any group that has an abundance of energy to ring doorbells, man the street corners and escort voters to the polls. Negroes in their demonstrations and voter registration campaigns have been acquiring excellent training in just these tasks. They also have discipline perhaps beyond that of any other group, because it has become a condition of survival. Consider the political power that would be generated if the million Americans who marched in 1963 also put their energy directly into the electoral process.

Already in some states and cities in the South a *de facto* alliance of Negro and sympathetic white voters has elected a new type of local official—nonintegrationist, but nonsegregationist too. As Negroes extend their important voting and registration campaigns and attain bloc-voting importance, such officials will move from dead center and slowly find the courage to stand unequivocally for integration.

Using Political Power

On the national scene the Congress today is dominated by Southern reactionaries whose control of the key committees enables them to determine legislation. Disenfranchisement of the Negro and the nonexercise of the vote by poor whites have permitted the Southern congressman to wrest his election from a tiny group, which he manipulates easily to return him again and again to office. United with Northern reactionaries, these unrepresentative legislators have crippled the country by blocking urgently needed action. Only with the growth of an enlightened electorate, white and Negro together, can we put a quick end to this century-old stranglehold of a minority on the nation's legislative processes.

There are those who shudder at the idea of a political bloc, particularly a Negro bloc, which conjures up visions of racial exclusiveness. This concern is, however, unfounded. Not exclusiveness but effectiveness is the aim of bloc voting; by forming a bloc, a minority makes its voice heard. The Negro minority will unite for political action for the same reason that it will seek to function in alliance with other groups—because in this way it can compel the majority to listen.

It is well to remember that blocs are not unique in American life, nor are they inherently evil. Their purposes determine their moral quality. In past years labor, farmers, businessmen, veterans and various national minorities have voted as blocs on various issues, and many still do. If the objectives are good and if each issue is decided on its own merits, a bloc is a wholesome force on the political scene. . . .

Because Negroes can quite readily become a compact, conscious and vigorous force in politics, they can do more than achieve their own racial goals. American politics needs nothing so much as an injection of the idealism, self-sacrifice and sense of public service which is the hallmark of our movement. . . .

One aspect of the civil rights struggle that receives little attention is the contribution it makes to the whole society. The Negro, in winning rights for himself, produces substantial benefits for the nation. Just as a doctor will occasionally reopen a wound because a dangerous infection hovers beneath the half-healed surface, the revolution for human rights is opening up unhealthy areas in American life and permitting a new and wholesome healing to take place. Eventually the civil rights movement will have contributed infinitely more to the nation than the eradication of racial injustice. It will have enlarged the concept of brotherhood to a vision of total interrelatedness. On that day, . . . John Donne's doctrine, "No man is an islande," will find its truest application in the United States.

In measuring the full implications of the civil rights revolution, the greatest contribution may be in the area of world peace. The concept of nonviolence has spread on a mass scale in the United States as an instrument of change in the field of race relations. To date, only a relatively few practitioners of nonviolent direct action have been committed to its philosophy. The great mass have used it pragmatically as a tactical weapon, without being ready to live it.

More and more people, however, have begun to conceive of this powerful ethic as a necessary way of life in a world where the wildly accelerated development of nuclear power has brought into being weapons that can annihilate all humanity. Political agreements are no longer secure enough to safeguard life against a peril of such devastating finality. There must also be a philosophy, acceptable to the people and stronger than resignation toward sudden death. . . .

Nonviolence, the answer to the Negroes' need, may become the answer to the most desperate need of all humanity.

A "MARSHALL PLAN" FOR THE AMERICAN NEGRO [4]

The National Urban League challenges the responsible leadership of our country to undertake a massive "Marshall Plan" approach program of intensified special effort to close the wide

[4] From "A Statement," by the Board of Trustees of the National Urban League, June 9, 1963. The National Urban League, Inc. 14 E. 48th St. New York, N.Y. 10017. '63. p 1-5. Reprinted by permission.

economic, social, and educational gap which separates the large majority of Negro citizens from other Americans.

Such special effort, which may appear to be in conflict with the principle of equal treatment for all, is required to overcome the damaging effects of generations of deprivation and denial and to make it possible for the majority of American Negroes to reach the point at which they can compete on a basis of equality in the nation's increasingly complex and fast-moving industrial economy.

The primary justification for such special effort lies in the fact that the nation itself is in jeopardy as long as it has within its body politic a large group of citizens who are socially and economically handicapped, often dependent, poorly educated, and unable to assume the normal responsibilities of citizenship. And with the impact of automation, it appears possible that these conditions will become worse before they improve and that we may well create a permanent class of dependents unable to make a useful contribution to our way of life.

The second reason for such an effort arises from the fact that the intense needs and problems which are evident in so many Negro communities around the country are a direct result of past and present discrimination and exclusion based on race. Thus, as a matter of historic equity, compensatory effort is justified and may well be the only means of overcoming the heavy aftermath of past neglect. As the following indices suggest, despite progress in certain areas, a large segment of the American Negro population continues to lag seriously behind other Americans in almost every type of measurement which can be used to determine social and economic well-being. And in certain categories the gap is widening rather than closing.

The median annual income for the Negro family today is $3,233 as compared with $5,835 for whites, a gap of 45 per cent. That the trend is in the wrong direction is evidenced by the fact that the gap in 1952 was 43 per cent. Hence, that one element in the gap has widened rather than narrowed in barely more than a decade.

More than 75 per cent of all Negro workers are found in the three lowest occupational categories—service workers, semiskilled and unskilled laborers, and farm workers. Less than 39 per cent of all white workers are in these categories. And these are the very categories which are being most drastically affected by automation.

One of every six Negro dwelling units in the nation is dilapidated, obsolete, or otherwise substandard, as compared to one in 32 white dwellings. In 1961 Negroes occupied 47 per cent of all public housing units in the country.

The lower earning power of Negro men and the more frequent breakup of Negro families make it necessary for more Negro than white women to become breadwinners. One in every four Negro women with preschool children is at work and not at home.

More Negro youth drop out of high school than white youth, and fewer high school graduates enter college. During the 1960 school year, 21 per cent of the school dropouts were Negroes. Of youth graduating from high school only 7 per cent were Negro youth.

Unemployment rates for Negroes are substantially higher than for whites at all ages: In 1961, 13 per cent of nonwhite men were unemployed as compared with 5.7 per cent of whites. Nationwide, Negro young people constitute only 15 per cent of the total youth population between the ages of sixteen and twenty-one, yet are 50 per cent of the youth population in this age bracket who are both out of school and unemployed.

To correct the problems indicated by these statistics, the cooperative effort of many social agencies, both public and private, in a massive "crash" attack on the problem is required. Such a crash program, sustained for a reasonable period of time, will realize savings of millions of dollars in the cost of welfare services and public hospitalization. Such a program will reverse the widespread social deterioration of urban families and communities and also help us develop the tools and understanding which will prevent the development of such deterioration in the future.

A Ten-Point Program

Specifically, what is involved in this kind of special effort which the Urban League now proposes?

(1) Our basic definition of equal opportunity must be broadened and deepened to include recognition of the need for

special effort to overcome serious disabilities resulting from historic handicaps.

(2) Our society must recognize and put a higher value than it has ever before placed on the human potential possessed by Negro citizens. And then it must move positively to develop that potential.

(3) The best schools and the best teachers are needed to prepare Negro children and other educationally disadvantaged youth to the point where they will have the desire for excellence in education and will be motivated to achieve and prepare to advance up the economic ladder with full realization of the rewards that will accrue in the process.

(4) Token integration and pilot placement in business and industry, labor, and government, are not enough. A conscious, planned effort must be made to place qualified Negroes in entrance jobs in all types of employment and in positions of responsibility, including lower and upper management positions.

(5) Affirmative action must be taken to destroy the racial ghetto and open housing opportunities of all types on the basis of need and ability to buy or rent.

(6) Public and private agencies in the health and welfare field must offer to the ghettoized segments of the population the best services, with highly competent personnel who understand the reasons for unstable family patterns, the relation between low socioeconomic status and social problems, and what must be done to rehabilitate urban Negro families.

(7) Qualified Negroes should be sought and named to all public and private boards and commissions, and particularly those which shape policy in the areas of employment, housing, education, and health and welfare services, the areas in which the racial differential is greatest and the need for dramatic change is most urgent. To achieve this objective, strong leadership within the Negro community must be developed. This leadership then will be ready to step into the vanguard of the teamwork effort demanded in resolving the smoldering problems involved in civil rights.

(8) Negro citizens themselves, adults as well as young people, must maintain and even accelerate the sense of urgency which now characterizes the drive for first-class citizenship. Every op-

portunity for the acquisition of education and technical skills must be utilized. Every means of strengthening the social and economic fabric of the Negro community must be employed.

(9) It is vital that government, philanthropic foundations, business, and industry reassess the extent of their financial support to establish organizations committed to securing equal opportunity for Negro citizens to share in the fundamental privileges and rights of American democracy. It is imperative that all of these major sources of financial support substantially increase their contributions to the preventive programs carried on by established, responsible Negro leadership organizations.

(10) Constructive efforts on the part of Negro citizens must be exerted to carry their full share of the responsibilities for participation in a meaningful way in every phase of community life.

The kinds of action set forth in the foregoing represent the only way in which significant breakthroughs on a broad scale can be accomplished. This is compensatory consideration in the form of inclusion, selection and preference.

The consequences of the "Negro revolt," as it has been characterized, are yet to be seen. It, therefore, behooves America's leadership to give serious consideration to a radical new approach by which the democracy we profess to practice is granted without further delay to all citizens.

NEGRO LEADERS SPEAK [5]

The struggle for civil rights for a tenth of the nation—the 20 million Negroes—is at a critical stage. The New York *Times Magazine* asked five major Negro leaders, who reflect a wide range of views, two basic questions:

Just what do you want?

How do you expect to achieve your goals?

In the interviews, one was made sharply aware of the fact that *all* of these leaders are angry men today.

The militant liberals:

Roy Wilkins, executive secretary of the National Association for the Advancement of Colored People, heads the largest and

[5] From "Five Angry Men Speak Their Minds," by Gertrude Samuels, staff writer, New York *Times*. New York *Times Magazine*. p 14+. My. 17, '64. © 1964 by The New York Times Company. Reprinted by permission.

the oldest (created in 1909) interracial, civil rights group in the country. JAMES FARMER, national director of the Congress of Racial Equality, has been arrested in the North and South for his direct-action protests. CORE, founded in 1942, achieved special prominence in 1960 following a wave of Southern sit-ins; it organized the Freedom Rides. BAYARD RUSTIN, an "independent" architect of demonstrations and boycotts who describes himself as a "democratic socialist," has also been in jail for civil disobedience. . . .

The extremists:

REPRESENTATIVE ADAM CLAYTON POWELL is chairman of the House Committee on Education and Labor. Powell supports the Reverend Milton Galamison. . . . The REVEREND MILTON GAL-AMISON, a Brooklyn minister, led two school boycotts (and lost the support of other Negro leaders in the process). . . . He has been accused of "nihilism" for asserting that he would prefer no public schools to segregated schools. . . .

What Do You Want?

WILKINS: The thing that we want immediately is the enactment of the Civil Rights Bill [Congress passed the bill in June 1964—Ed.]. We are concerned with jobs, education, housing. But because the passage of this bill reaffirms the dignity that you collect as a human being, as a result of legislation, it's as valuable from that standpoint as the specific evils that it seeks to correct. The main trouble thus far has been a piecemeal approach—a sip from a long-handled spoon now and then to keep the Negro people quiescent.

We've been given large doses of the "great progress that has been made," and the most irritating of all has been the assertion that "you are so much better off than any other Negroes in the world." The contrast is made with the Bantu of South Africa or the Congolese. This is nonsense. The true comparison is: How does the Negro compare with other Americans? . . .

FARMER: We want jobs, housing and quality integrated education—and we want them *now*. White liberals must realize that the dues in this movement are getting higher all the time—not in terms of money but in terms of involvement. The trouble with the North is that words and pious platitudes have taken the place of action. It is no accident that the issue of schools has become a key issue. Negroes are now fighting for their children. Without quality education, their children—born and unborn—can never hope to participate fully in the nation's economic, social and political life.

The fundamental thing is for the Negro to be accepted as a human being—and for the North to stop making the Negro the Invisible Man. (Farmer was referring to Ralph Ellison's phrase, in his award-winning novel *Invisible Man,* to dramatize the Negro's dilemma in a white man's world: "I am an invisible man. No, I am not a spook like those who haunted Edgar Allan Poe. . . . I am a man of substance, of flesh and bone, fiber and liquids— and I might even be said to possess a mind. I am invisible, understand, simply because people refuse to see me. . . . When they approach me they see only my surroundings, themselves, or figments of their imagination—indeed, everything and anything except me.") The Northerner tries to forget the Negro and sweep him under the rug. Negroes have been hidden away in slum ghettos. A visitor can come to almost any Northern city—and unless he takes a guided tour, he will not see the Negro. We want the North to realize that passing a law—and in the North there are good laws on the books—does not solve the problem. The laws have to be enforced.

Slumlords are taken to court, ordered by the court to clean up the violations, and the slumlords defy the court. If the slumlords can't do the job, then the city must take it over and do it. Of course this will cost money—but not nearly so much as the rising anger in the Negro community will cost.

RUSTIN: I want the right for the Negro fully to share the freedom, responsibilities and the obligations of this society. Whites are more deeply affected than Negroes, because there are more whites. Whites do not understand that their own freedom, economic and social, is gravely curtailed because the Negro doesn't have his. People get excited at the stall-ins and sit-ins at the World's Fair. Why don't they get excited about the destruction to democracy, which is the Southern filibuster in the Senate? [Senate debate on the main body of the Civil Rights Bill opened on March 30, 1964, and continued until cloture was voted on June 10.—Ed] I want the fight to go beyond segregation and discrimination, and I want to build allies with labor, with church forces and with liberals, to demand the following five-point program:

Full employment; national economic planning; to train people within this planning for existing jobs; a Federal subsidy for education, which is our most important "industry" today; and, finally a $30 billion works program to help absorb the unskilled Negro labor. Here's where the Negro comes in. Being the least skilled he could first be put to work helping to construct these new roads, schools, hospitals; then be trained to take his place as a permanent worker inside those institutions.

The Extremists Speak

POWELL: I want immediate desegregation, North and South. This means that in the school system there should be immediate busing in and busing out of the black neighborhoods. In employment, I want upgrading and retraining for Negroes; and legislation for the school dropouts and pushouts—those youngsters who don't qualify for graduation. And there should be preferential hiring.

The preferential hiring and the busing should be seen as temporary methods—perhaps lasting five years—until the long-range programs go into effect. If two people apply for a job and one is black and one is white and both have the same qualities, I say, hire the black man. Preferential hiring is just, until a reasonable percentage of jobs for Negroes has been arrived at.

I reject emphatically the idea that the atmosphere of Washington, with a Civil Rights Bill, can inspire the country. The bill will not be meaningful to two thirds of the Negroes. . . .

The black man has come to the conclusion that the white man has "given" all he is going to give, and that what he needs now he must fight for. The "Black Revolution" is now led by blacks. For years, the white liberals, with their specially chosen black liberals—not all of whom were truly liberal—monopolized the civil rights movement. The Negro is casting off the smothering mantle of paternalism.

I think there should be one place set aside in Harlem where white people wait on Negroes.

GALAMISON: I want the tangible gains in this order of their importance: quality, integrated education—a real first step toward the resolution of all the other problems; then jobs—there is always a constant struggle for equal job opportunity; then housing —and the rent strike idea is symptomatic of the dissatisfaction in housing, rent gouging and exploitation.

The kind of complete acceptance and complete equality that the Negro wants, and that everyone should have, will come as the by-product of the gains in these other tangible areas.

What I am trying to say is that you can't *make* another fellow like you. But the fact that he may not like you does not give him the license to deprive you of your basic rights. It's the basic rights we're after. The point is, this struggle is not just an effort to save the Negro people. The health and survival of the nation depend on how the struggle is handled. Meaning that I just don't feel that this country has any future at all if it doesn't resolve this race problem.

How Do You Expect to Achieve Your Goals?

WILKINS: There is no one method which will accomplish the goals all over the United States for all the Negroes of the United States. What may be effective in Boston is not effective in Biloxi. A conference may be used here, a lawsuit or political action to attain legislative goals there; in another place, it may be community education, a boycott, a picket line, or moral suasion through churches.

We are now, for instance, using in one city an economic boycott—a buyers' strike—with the result that more than half a dozen stores have been forced to close in a certain shopping area. It was largely the women of this community who brought this off —without flamboyance—a committee of women directing the telephone campaign and doorbell ringing. There were no mass meetings, no marches, no pickets—but for that community it was the right weapon: the quiet boycott.

We are convinced that solutions also depend on strengthening the Negro population from within. Thus several NAACP chapters are tutoring students, to help them overcome the lags brought about by deprivation.

We reject violent aggression. We definitely believe that the organization of rifle clubs, assertedly "for defense" as Malcolm X announced, not only is an aggressive act but is a positive encouragement to violence and bloodshed.

FARMER: We will achieve our goals by making the Negro *visible* through demonstrations. We hope to achieve it by grass-roots organizing in the Negro ghettos, around such tactics of non-cooperation as the rent strike and the boycott. Another strategy will be to form alliances with the oppressed minorities, such as the Puerto Ricans, Mexican-Americans, American Indians and others. And by forming alliances with unemployed and depressed workers, such as migratory and farm labor—in other words, joining the war on poverty and giving it motivation and drive.

Employed white workers, through their trade unions, must line up with this struggle. Middle-class whites should join the movement by supporting the economic and school boycotts, and by participating in the demonstrations.

In the past year in the North, we have been demanding action. Instead of action, we've gotten bureaucratic red tape and more delays. We're angry. But I think anger can be a very creative thing. The nation didn't start to move on this problem at all until masses of Negroes became angry.

RUSTIN: I am for any form of Negro movement—in the streets —which is nonviolent in character. The Negro must stay in the streets, because for the past ten years, all social movement in the country has sprung from the Negro challenge. Mrs. Rosa Parks sat down in the front of that bus in Montgomery, Alabama, back in 1955—a sort of mother of the modern social revolution. Her protest was followed by the sit-in movement and the Freedom Ride movement.

Why stay in the streets? Because there is nowhere else to have movement. American society is traditionally moved in response to action in the streets, what I call "social dislocation." This is the way that the women got the vote back in he early 1900's— by picketing and forming human chains and marching in the streets and by going to jail. This is the way that the labor unions were taken seriously, back in the 1930's, when they went into the streets in Detroit, Chicago, New York and into strikes against capitalists who fought them. The Negro must follow this American tradition.

The second strategy is to project the five-point economic program into Congress, into business, and also into the streets. There should be demonstrations in the legislatures, against mayors and governors, as well as marches on construction sites and against labor unions and others which discriminate. My formula against a long and bloody summer is to have vigorous action around the political conventions. This will absorb the frustration that has been building up in the Negro people, in creative and positive action.

It's not just a civil rights program any more—otherwise, Negroes and whites will fight each other over the few jobs that are available. It's a program of self-interest—where thoughtful whites must join with the Negroes.

POWELL: We must use every tactic available, short of violence —demonstrations, picketing, boycotts, selective buying. Demonstrations must and will increase.

I was deeply concerned when Brother Malcolm X was quoted in the press, regarding Negroes arming themselves. I discussed this with him. He said he was incorrectly quoted. He said to me that "in those areas of the United States where the Negro had no protection whatsoever, he was then duty-bound to see that in his home he had guns with which to protect himself." If this is his correct statement, then I agree with him. Self-defense is the great American tradition—a man's home is his castle. He should be armed in his home, for the protection of his home, in the North and in the South.

Our United States is spiraling downward at such a momentum that I doubt whether it can be saved. Too many white people in this nation would rather want America destroyed than give equality to black people. The United States is finished as a great power of the world unless it satisfies the minimum expectations of the "Black Revolution."

We are witnessing a revolution of the black masses, as was clearly brought out at the meeting of the Northern demonstration leaders, known as ACT [a new group which has denounced the Civil Rights Bill and the old Negro leadership]. ACT has asked me to be their consultant, and at sixty years of age I'll be the grand old man of the "Black Revolution."

GALAMISON: There isn't any blueprint to achieve our aims. The situation will have to be played pretty much by ear. Much of what happens will not depend on the Negro. It will depend on the action or the inaction of the whites.

I feel we will do whatever is necessary to be done. This means that if we cannot achieve these inalienable rights by the kind of efforts now practiced—demonstrations, sit-ins, stall-ins, picket lines—we will have to think of other tactics.

No Negroes are exercising violence, and those who seem to be most concerned about violence ought to clean up the mess, then we wouldn't have to worry about violence as a possibility. I think that if people are against rifle clubs for Negroes, then they should be against rifle clubs for all people. If people have never raised their voices in oppsition to a white group forming a rifle club, but are only opposed to Negroes having rifle clubs then here is where prejudice creeps in. I don't want to get into this discussion about violence. If you're suggesting that equality is going to be achieved without a struggle, I can't see it.

I would say that if these problems are not resolved in a civilized way, then anything can happen.

IS EQUALITY ENOUGH IN EDUCATION? [6]

The temptation is always strong to say that the Negro child should be seen merely as any other child, respected as an individual, and provided with an educational program that will best meet his particular combination of needs. Of course the Negro child, like any other child, is entitled to be treated as an individual. Such treatment is the only sound basis for projecting his or any other child's education, but the easy generalization does not always come to grips with the whole truth.

The American Negro youngster happens to be a member of a large and distinctive group that for a very long time has been the object of special political, legal, and social action. This, I remind you, is not a question of what should be true, or might have

[6] From "Educational Problems of Segregation and Desegregation," by John H. Fischer, president of Teachers College, Columbia University. A chapter in *Education in Depressed Areas,* edited by A. Harry Passow. Bureau of Publications, Teachers College, Columbia University. New York. '63. p 291-6. © 1963 by Teachers College, Columbia University. Reprinted by permission.

been, but an undeniable and inescapable fact. To act as though any child is suddenly separable from his history is indefensible. In terms of educational planning, it is also irresponsible.

Every Negro child is the victim of the history of his race in this country. On the day he enters kindergarten, he carries a burden no white child can ever know. . . . We are dealing here with no ordinary question of intercultural understanding although cultural difference is part of the difficulty. Nor are we concerned with only the usual range of psycho-educational problems, for the psychological situation of the Negro child is affected by quite special social considerations.

I recognize the hazard in speaking of "the Negro child." It is equally unsatisfactory to speak of "the white child" or "the Puerto Rican child" or "the Spanish-American child" as though any child could be encompassed in a stereotype. Whatever a child's ethnic or racial background, he may be bright or slow, attractive or unpleasant; his parents may be rich or poor, well educated or illiterate, responsible or shiftless. Every racial group distributes itself in some fashion over the whole social and economic scale. But when all the variability is conceded, it cannot be denied that every American Negro child must expect to encounter certain problems which none of our other children face in quite the same way. . . .

Many of the Negro children who now come to school are the victims of their parents' lack of knowledge and of schooling. The parents in turn are the victims of a situation over which they have had little or no control themselves. Parents and children alike elicit sympathy and attract charity, but praiseworthy as these responses may be, they form no adequate approach to the education of the disadvantaged urban child. The response of the community and the school must be based also on objective knowledge and mature understanding of the underlying difficulty and an inventive turn of mind among teachers and administrators. Teaching reading, for example, to a first-grade child who has never seen an adult read anything requires an approach quite different from one appropriate to a child in whose home books are as normal as food.

Similarly, a child who has never known sustained conversation with his parents must actually learn the skills of continuing discussion before he can learn much else in school. . . .

In respect to the development of intellectual competence, many Negro children face special problems. . . . During years of oppression, first under slavery and later under more subtle forms of discrimination, the opportunities for large numbers of Negroes to apply their own rational powers with initiative and freedom to important problems have been far more limited than the opportunities available to other racial groups. Many Negro children, therefore, carry the disabling scars of the culture in which they were nurtured, a culture which encouraged the use of muscles and not only discouraged but often penalized those who sought to use their minds creatively. The school must take all of this into account and build programs and provide opportunities which not only reflect these facts but move aggressively to *compensate* for them. . . .

This implication for policy and practice cuts more than one way, however, for just as certainly as no person should be subjected to discriminatory treatment which depresses him because of his race, so it follows that none should be given preferential treatment simply because his complexion or his ancestry is different from another's. A practical application of this principle may arise if a school organizes classes according to the academic ability of students. If . . . it should develop that one classroom contains pupils largely of one racial group while a second classroom is composed mostly of another, the school should not be criticized for the result. If, on the other hand, the school authorities have used an ostensibly educational device simply to justify some predetermined racial arrangement, the action is totally indefensible. . . .

A second guideline for the development of policy and practice centers about the concept of equality of opportunity. "Equality of opportunity" . . . means much more than a schoolroom desk for every child. It connotes, rather, a condition in which every American may rightfully expect to find himself in fair competition with every other American. This condition is achieved and maintained by the operation of a host of agencies and forces, some political, some social, others economic or cultural. . . .

In the cases of some Americans, and in that of the Negro American most dramatically, our traditional system has failed for a long time in countless ways to provide that equality of opportunity that should be the condition of all our people. . . . Especially is this true of children whose parents and grandparents were deliberately, systematically, and by law denied what is now clearly recognized as fully equal treatment.

Is it not a reasonable contention—and a just one—that to compensate for past injustice, we should offer these children educational services beyond the level of what might be called standard equality?

Could it be that to achieve total equality of opportunity in America we may have to modify currently accepted ideas about equality of opportunity. . . ? Is it conceivable that some of our children are entitled to more and better eduactional opportunities than most of the others? In fact, of course, the question has already been answered. Thousands of mentally and physically handicapped children, regardless of race, regularly receive teaching service, physical facilities, and supporting services more extensive and more costly than those furnished children who are considered physically and mentally normal. In the cases of many Negro children—and the generalization would apply also to certain other minority groups—we may need to substitute for our traditional concept of equal educational opportunity a new concept of *compensatory opportunity*. . . .

I doubt that anyone is in a position now to say precisely what the concept of compensatory educational opportunity would mean in every case, but my purpose here is not so much to answer the question as to raise it for discussion. The concept of compensatory opportunity should certainly not be restricted to any one group and, as I have suggested, it has already been applied to other types of disability. But, to the degree that a child's race or cultural background handicap him, and especially where they are attributable, at least in part, to earlier governmental action, they should be taken into account in adjusting his educational program.

EQUALITY FOR BOTH NEGROES AND WHITES [7]

The "Negro problem" does not involve the Negro alone; it is a problem facing the whole country. For 350 years, white

[7] From "The Negro's Problem Is the White's," by Eli Ginzberg, professor of economics at Columbia University and director of its Conservation of Human Resources project. New York *Times Magazine.* p 14+. F. 9, '64. © 1964 by The New York Times Company. Reprinted by permission.

America has stood the Negro off. Why it did so, and with what consequences, are lessons we should study carefully.

During World War II, I found that many senior members of the military—intelligent men with whom I had daily dealings—seemed to have different views of the Negro from mine. In searching for an explanation, I realized many of these officers were from the South. They had grown up during the early years of the century, and their image of the Negro was still a reflection of the one they acquired in youth. I, on the other hand, came from a Northern state. All of us, therefore, Northerners as well as Southerners, are prisoners of time and perspective. Even the effective leaders of today's Negro protest movement sometimes act as if history began yesterday. The real challenge is to broaden and deepen our perspective beyond the limits of our own individual experience.

The first conclusion to be derived from history is that our democracy, by conception and commitment, was a white democracy only. The Negro was excluded from the Declaration of Independence and from the Constitution. The Great Abolitionist, William Lloyd Garrison, was right when he said that, from this point of view, the Constitution was "a pact with the devil." The Negro was counted out. Much of the intractable difficulty American democracy has experienced with respect to the Negro citizen, therefore, comes from having to restructure its basic institutions to make room for him. Gunnar Myrdal, the distinguished Swedish economist and author of the first comprehensive study of the Negro, *An American Dilemma,* was wrong, in my opinion, when he said that there has been a conflict between our convictions and our actions. He complimented us, because he misunderstood the problem. We never had a commitment, as a nation, to the Negro.

The Constitution—the basic law of the land—dealt with the Negro in three ways: first, it stipulated that Congress could put an end to the slave trade but not before 1808; second, it authorized the Federal Government to return runaway slaves to their owners; and, third, it provided that a slave would be counted as three-fifths of a man in determining the basis of representation in the House of Representatives—hardly the type of legislation to justify Myrdal's belief that we had a democratic commitment to the Negro. [See "Negroes and the Civil Rights Laws," Section II, below.] A further piece of evidence is that no President of the

United States from George Washington to William Howard Taft
had any answer to the problem presented by Negroes in white
America except to suggest, in one way or another, that they leave
the country.

The South Versus the North and West

The second historical fact is that although the Negro has
mostly lived in the South, the North and the West have also
been, and remain, generally hostile to him. . . .

The South has never had the determining voice. The destiny
of the Negro in America has always been shaped primarily by the
attitudes and actions of white citizens in the North and West,
who were not interested in the Negro and made no commitments
to him. As early as the drafting of the Constitution, and many
times thereafter, the North said to the South: "We will not interfere in your relationships with the Negro if you will not interfere
with some of our basic economic policies."

The third conclusion from history is that such gains as Negroes have been able to make usually came when whites did not
have to pay for them—or when they wanted something from the
Negro or from each other. Negro slaves had a chance to win
their freedom during the Revolutionary War when the British
offered to free all those who would fight for them. George Washington, who had at first refused to take Negroes into the army,
then permitted them to enlist. Later, when North and South
engaged in fratricidal war, Lincoln himself said that he would
settle the war gladly even if he could not free a single Negro.
He believed his primary responsibility as Chief Executive was to
settle the war; emancipation was merely a military expedient.

It is only since 1940, when the North needed and wanted
Negro labor in pursuit of the defense effort and of economic
growth, that the Negro has begun to make significant gains.
When the country finally needed Negro manpower, Negroes were
able to advance as citizens.

The New Deal was established because President Roosevelt
was concerned about the problems of the handicapped third of
the population—the people who were badly fed, badly housed
and had no work. Under his leadership, we were able to establish Federal programs that incidentally embraced the Negro. Not
all of them provided him with significant benefits, however.

Those measures that required the cooperation of the states and local areas—such as the agricultural programs—were of limited advantage to the Negro. But where Federal power was exercised in programs like Social Security, unemployment insurance and public works, the Negro enjoyed the benefits equally.

History thus points to two conclusions: that animosity, indifference and neglect have characterized the attitude of the white population toward the Negro in both the North and the South; and that most of the Negro's progress to date has been made through the economic self-interest of the white community rather than through its active encouragement.

The Plight of White and Black

How, then, do we stand now—and what are the prospects? Despite the fact that Negroes are more urbanized today than the white population (roughly 75 per cent live in urban communities), the rural South remains the center of poverty, unemployment, underemployment, undereducation and racialism in its most aggravated forms.

One and a half million Negroes left the South in the 1950's but despite that tremendous migration, there will have to be another one soon. There is no future for *all* the whites and Negroes who still remain on Southern farms. Dr. C. E. Bishop of North Carolina State College of Agriculture and Engineering has estimated that of the million and a half young people between the ages of ten and twenty still employed on the land in the South, only 150,000 will be needed by the end of the decade. President Kennedy made much the same calculation in his manpower report. He stated that only about one in ten of the young people now growing up in the farm areas of the United States—and an even smaller percentage in the South—had a chance of making a living in agriculture.

These poorly educated, poorly trained whites and Negroes naturally gravitate toward the large cities. But urban areas that used to be so hospitable to new arrivals and offered a place for anyone with a strong back, are no longer conglomerations of first-generation immigrants—they have become third- and fourth-generation middle-class communities. The yawning gap between these farm migrants and the cities' residents makes for an entirely new source of social tension.

Even those Negroes who have started up the income and occupational scale—who escaped to the cities in the 1940's and did well in the wartime and postwar booms—are in trouble. They are heavily concentrated in those sectors of the economy that are most affected by automation and technological change—on Detroit assembly lines, in Chicago meat-packing plants and the steel mills of Pittsburgh. These are the industries where semiskilled laborers are being squeezed out—and Negroes loom very large in their ranks.

At the height of the Korean War, unemployment among Negroes was approximately 4 per cent—considerably below the level in the work force as a whole in recent years. Today, the level of Negro unemployment is 11 to 12 per cent or even higher.

Another element in the problem is that the Negro birth rate is now considerably above the white birth rate—for many reasons, including improvements in health and consequent reductions in sterility. This comes at a time when the number of young people available for work is already increasing phenomenally and both white and Negro youngsters are having more and more difficulty finding jobs.

Despite this gloomy picture, however, there is one encouraging piece of evidence. In both North and South, a growing minority of Negroes have managed to climb up the economic and occupational ladder. In Chicago, for instance, 30 per cent of the Negro families have a higher income than 50 per cent of the white families. In the West, the nonwhite income distribution is almost the exact counterpart of income distribution among the white population of the South.

The Economics of Inequality

This suggests that our complicated, diffuse and widely differentiated society offers many options, many ways to go around obstacles, that permit members of disadvantaged minorities to escape from the slough.

Nevertheless, the general drift of the economy and the rapid increase in the labor force do present a formidable problem for an underprivileged group. One crucial index makes this clear: In the last ten years approximately 800,000 new jobs have been created annually; but even without reducing the present level of unemployment—which is much too high—we need half as many again each year just to absorb the tremendous increase in the number of youngsters coming of working age.

And, despite a growing national income, there is nothing on the horizon at the moment to inspire much confidence in our ability to achieve this aim. President Johnson recently emphasized the rapid gains that the economy had made during the past two and a half years: $100 billion more in gross national product, and 2.5 million more jobs. But put these figures together and they show that it took $40 billion of additional GNP [gross national product] to create one million additional jobs!

What bearing do these economic and manpower trends have on the strategy and tactics of the civil rights movement? So far, the great contribution of the protest movement has been to underscore, first for the Negro and then for the white community, that the Negro must become a full partner in an America that historically had no place for him and no commitment to receive him. The protest movement has said plainly that all Negroes must have all of the rights—civil and political—that were conferred by three constitutional amendments after the Civil War but which were never adequately enforced.

But no minority can bring about this desired end by itself. Power in a democracy rests with the majority. Against a backdrop of white animosity or lack of interest, the only answer is to find potential allies for the Negroes among the poor, the ill-educated, the unemployed and the menially employed (together, a considerable part of the white community), as well as the Spanish-speaking community and some other minority groups.

Allies, however, come at a price. In the perspective of our democratic tradition, it appears that if a minority's program is to gain the support of others, it must somehow serve their needs as well as its own.

The Economics of Equality

It becomes important, therefore, to determine what white America is willing to do for white Americans—and thus incidentally for the Negro.

Approached in this light, the history of the new federalism from Roosevelt to Johnson seems to indicate that if acceptable programs can be found for improvements in education, health and welfare, and for urban renewal, all those in need of special Government help in these areas will have a chance to get it.

Education alone is too slow an answer to the Negroes' problem. It is necessary to move along on the educational front, but the real emergency is in the employment situation. We have—on the books—a congressional commitment to full employment passed in 1946 with the strong support of both parties, but it has never been fully impemented.

To revive the Employment Act of 1946 would be a major attack on racialism, and there is a good possibility of its political success because there are even more white youngsters who need a chance to work than Negro youngsters. If this were done, we would then have short-run job and long-run educational programs supporting each other. A balance must be found among multiple programs—those which Negroes should attempt to accomplish largely on their own (such as protest and civil rights); objectives, like improved welfare and rehabilitation programs, which they must work toward in alliance with others, and full employment, which is a challenge to all groups in our society.

In the absence of such a program, however, it would be understandable if large parts of the Negro community chose to give up the struggle, as the Black Muslims have suggested, and withdraw, either physically or spiritually, from America. It would be understandable if their despair reached the point of total alienation.

But I believe that the trials, suffering and victories of Negro men, women and children over the last 350 years have not been in vain. It has taken the nation much too long to admit the Negro to full citizenship, but we are at last on the threshold of establishing a biracial society based on freedom and equality for all. It is late but it is also early, for no other nation has ever attempted this.

II. THE ROLE OF LAW AND GOVERNMENT

EDITOR'S INTRODUCTION

The decade 1954-1964 culminated in the passage of the Civil Rights Act of 1964. It is a law comparable in many ways with similar legislation enacted after the Civil War which was, however, nullified in practice and by the courts. The first selection below recalls that period in light of the present action regarding civil rights. This is followed by a brief summary of the new 1964 Civil Rights Act and excerpts from an article by Alexander M. Bickel, professor of law at Yale University, which analyzes the new law and its significance in more detail.

The Government's role in civil rights is illustrated by two presidential speeches. The first was made by President John F. Kennedy when he submitted the Civil Rights Bill to Congress in June 1963; the second was delivered by President Lyndon B. Johnson a little more than a year later when he was about to sign the act into law. Both will go down in history as the first such forthright statements on behalf of Negro civil rights by any of America's Presidents. They are followed by the speech in opposition to the Civil Rights Bill, then before the Senate, by Senator Barry M. Goldwater of Arizona, the 1964 Republican party presidential candidate. Next the editor and publisher of the Atlanta *Constitution,* Ralph McGill, looks ahead to the prospects for equal opportunities for Negroes in the South and finds that the achievement of voting rights will mainly determine that future.

Underlining the fact that laws do not always determine behavior, the concluding articles in the section are devoted to three themes: first, that more than the passage of a law is needed to correct the injustices which Negroes have suffered; second, that in a state such as Mississippi the new law may have little effect unless there is Federal intervention; and third that, whatever the law, it may be necessary to reform the lower Federal court system and its personnel in the South if segregation is to be overcome.

NEGROES AND THE CIVIL RIGHTS LAWS [1]

The Emancipation Proclamation as a legally enforceable document was a nullity. It did not free the slaves.

In the first place, it was intended to free only those slaves in states or parts of states which, on January 1, 1863, were still in rebellion against the United States. Slavery in the nonrebellious states retained its previous legal status. In those states which were still rebellious, the Union forces were not in control and consequently the presidential freedom edict could not be enforced.

Moreover, the President's power to free the slaves was vulnerable on constitutional grounds. The Constitution, at that time, classified slaves as property and protected the slaveholders' rights to this property. The Proclamation had been issued by Lincoln pursuant to his constitutionally delegated war powers, the use of which, in this instance, violated "sacred" property rights.

Furthermore, in 1857, just six years earlier, the United States Supreme Court, in a five-to-four decision in the *Dred Scott* case, held that under the Constitution even a free Negro who had formerly been a slave had no rights which the white man was bound to respect. In other words, even a free Negro was no better off, legally speaking, than a slave. Consequently, when President Lincoln signed the Emancipation Proclamation, that particular stroke of a presidential pen amounted to no more than this nation's first official commitment to release the slaves from human bondage.

When the Civil War ended two years after the Proclamation's issuance, and the slaves were physically set free where Union forces were firmly in control, the Proclamation's constitutional validity remained in doubt. The Abolitionists, the Radical Republicans and Lincoln were determined to erase forever all such doubts. And so, as Lincoln put it: "The abolition of slavery by constitutional provision settles the fate, for all coming time, not only of millions now in bondage, but of unborn millions to come."

Thus on January 31, 1865, the "Ayes" had it. The Thirteenth Amendment passed the House. Three fourths of the states hav-

[1] From "The Constitution—Key to Freedom," by New York State Senator Constance Baker Motley, associate counsel of the NAACP Legal Defense and Educational Fund, Inc. *Ebony.* 28:221-6. S. '63. Reprinted by permission.

ing ratified the amendment, slavery was abolished on American soil by constitutional mandate December 18, 1865.

Then, four million former slaves looked at a constitutionally secure freedom—all men without a country. Chief Justice [Roger Brooke] Taney's decision in the *Dred Scott Case* was still the law of the land. According to that decision, these newly emancipated slaves could not lay claim to citizenship, their freedom not withstanding. Neither the Emancipation Proclamation nor the Thirteenth Amendment had conferred citizenship on their beneficiaries.

The Abolitionists would not rest. The Radical Republicans in the Congress found the answer—a new amendment to the Constitution. On July 28, 1868, the Fourteenth Amendment conferred national and state citizenship on "All persons born or naturalized in the United States, and subject to the jurisdiction thereof."

The states were also prohibited by the first section of this amendment from abridging the privileges and immunities of citizens of the United States and were prohibited from depriving any *person* of life, liberty, or property, without due process of law. Finally, the states were prohibited by this first section from denying to any *person* within their jurisdiction "the equal protection of the laws." On this clause, now known as the equal protection clause of the amendment, was to be hung all the law on civil rights. Section 5 of the Fourteenth Amendment conferred upon the Congress power to enforce its provisions by appropriate legislation—and this Charles Sumner [United States Senator from Massachusetts, 1851-1874] and other Radical Republicans in the Congress were determined to do.

But soon many representatives became convinced of the necessity for a constitutional amendment guaranteeing the right of of Negroes to vote; and so, on March 30, 1870, the Secretary of State proclaimed the ratification of the Fifteenth Amendment prohibiting the states, as well as the United States, from abridging the right to vote "on account of race, color or previous condition of servitude." Congress was also given power to enforce this amendment by appropriate legislation.

One of the Fourteenth Amendment's first progenies came on May 31, 1870, when the Congress enacted a law securing to "All *persons* within the jurisdiction of the United States . . . the same right in every state and territory to make and enforce contracts, to sue, be parties, give evidence, and to the full and equal benefit of all laws and proceedings for the security of persons and property as is enjoyed by white citizens." This law also required that all persons be subjected "to like punishment, pains, penalties, taxes, licenses and exactions of every kind, and to no other."

On April 9, 1866, following the adoption of the Thirteenth Amendment, the Congress had conferred upon all citizens of the United States "the same right in every State and Territory as is enjoyed by white citizens thereof to inherit, purchase, lease, sell, hold and convey real and personal property." Because of the doubtful constitutional validity of this law, it was reenacted by the Congress following adoption of the citizenship amendment.

On April 20, 1871, Congress, again in its determination to enforce the provisions of the Fourteenth Amendment, provided that: "Every person who, under color of any statute, ordinance, regulation, custom, or usage, of any State or Territory, subject, or causes to be subjected, any citizen of the United States or other persons within the jurisdiction thereof, to the deprivation of any rights, privileges or immunities secured by the Constitution and laws, shall be liable to the party injured in an action at law, suit in equity, or other proper proceedings for redress."

Many other civil rights laws were enacted during this period, but these three legislative creatures of the Reconstruction Congress are the bulwarks of civil rights actions in the courts today.

In 1874 when Charles Sumner lay dying in Massachusetts, he was still attempting to get through the Congress a bill securing equal rights for Negroes in public schools, cemeteries, on common carriers, in inns, in theaters and other places of public amusement. Sumner, who was perhaps the greatest champion of Negro rights, firmly believed that with the enactment of this bill, Congress would have established in law all the protection necessary to secure the rights of the nation's new body of citizens.

John R. Lynch, a Negro congressman from Mississippi, made a brilliant speech on the floor of the Congress in 1875 in support of the constitutionality of Sumner's proposed bill during the course of which he said: "No, Mr. Speaker, it is not social rights that we desire. We have enough of that already. What we ask is freedom in the enjoyment of public rights. Rights which are, or should be accorded to every citizen alike."

Mr. Rainey, another Negro representative from South Carolina, also supported Sumner's deathbed effort. He said to the Congress:

The condition of the colored race reminds me forcibly of what is said of Mohammed's coffin, which is affirmed to be oscillating between heaven and earth. The passage of this bill, the purpose of which is to accord equal rights to my race, who have felt and are still feeling the sad necessity for the same, will go further to allay the restive public sentiment in this regard and define more definitely the status of us, the new-born citizens, than any statutory enactment that has yet taken place.

The Law of 1875

Before this act passed the Congress, the provisions as to schools and cemeteries were stricken, but its passage meant that Negroes could ride on public transportational facilities, secure hotel accommodations and enter theaters and other places of amusement free from discrimination on account of color.

This law, enacted by the Congress in 1875, was declared unconstitutional by the United States Supreme Court in an eight-to-one decision in the *Civil Rights Cases* of 1883. The Court, in America's first great civil rights retreat ruled that the Fourteenth Amendment gave no protection to Negroes against the discriminatory refusal of a common carrier, an inn-keeper or owner of a theater to admit him thereto. The amendment, the court ruled, is a shield against the state only.

Seven years before, in 1876, the Radical Republicans were defeated in their bid for reelection to the Congress. but their legislative task had been completed. Virtually every civil right enjoyed by white citizens had been secured in law for the newly emancipated slaves. But the decision of 1883 was ominous. By this time, the North had lost interest in the perennial "Negro question" which had occupied so much of the Congress' time following the Civil War. And, as the historians tell us, the Hayes-Tilden Compromise of 1876, which made Rutherford Hayes (Republican of Ohio) the nineteenth President of these United States although Samuel Tilden (Democrat of New York) had won the popular vote, was a political deal whereby Republican politicians agreed to let the former slaveholders regain control of Southern state governments in exchange for disputed electoral Southern votes for Hayes. As a result, the Reconstruction state governments were replaced by disenfranchising the Negro and other illegal practices.

This was followed, in 1896, by the great legal compromise on the question of equal rights for Negroes. The Supreme Court, again in an eight-to-one decision (Mr. Justice [John Marshall] Harlan [1833-1911] . . . dissenting) upheld the doctrine of "separate but equal." It took fifty-eight years to redeem Charles Sumner's legacy.

In 1954, in the *School Segregation* cases, the Supreme Court finally held "separate but equal" unconstitutional as applied to education. This was the second Emancipation Proclamation.

By May 17, 1954, when the United States Supreme Court unanimously held racial segregation in public schools unconstitutional, prior NAACP-sponsored Supreme Court decisions had re-established for Negro Americans most of the rights which the post-Civil War Congress intended to secure when it proposed the adoption of the Thirteenth, Fourteenth and Fifteenth Amendments and enacted the civil rights legislation referred to above. The right to vote in the crucial primary elections in the South as well as in general elections had been secured. Ordinances passed by Southern cities restricting the areas in which Negroes might live had been held void. Systematic exclusion of Negroes from grand and petit juries in criminal cases had been prohibited. Racial segregation on interstate buses and railroads had been struck down. White property owners could no longer obtain court enforcement of racially restrictive covenants or damages for the breach of same. Approximately two thousand Negro students in the Southern and border states had been admitted to institutions of higher learning as a result of prior Supreme Court decisions. And lower Federal court decisions had equalized the salaries of Negro teachers. In short, by 1954 a long list of court decisions had gradually brought the Negro citizen close to the post-Civil War Congress' goal of equality with white citizens.

New Targets Set

With the Supreme Court's decision holding racial segregation in public schools unconstitutional, Negro citizens then turned their attention to other areas in which equal public status with white citizens was still denied. Since the Supreme Court's school desegregation decision of 1954, segregation in public recreational facilities (including swimming pools, parks and golf courses), public housing, and intrastate travel has been held unconstitutional. Moreover, recent court decisions have held that when these publicly owned facilities, including theaters and restaurants, are leased by a state or municipality to private persons for operation, such lessees may not discriminate on account of race and color. By 1960 when student sit-ins at privately owned lunch counters commenced, virtually every pubicly owned facility had been opened, in law, to the Negro on a basis of equality with whites. . . .

[Subsequent to the writing of this article, the 1964 Civil Rights Act was passed by Congress. It represents in many ways a reenactment of the Civil Rights Act of 1875.—Ed.]

It must not be forgotten that civil rights progress was reversed by the Supreme Court's decision of 1883 and its adoption of the "separate but equal" doctrine of 1896. As a result, segregation and racial discrimination have become so firmly entrenched in the deep South that it appears, at times, ineluctable. Its eradication has required even the use of Federal troops. And it appears that Federal trops will be required in the future to enforce Federal court desegregation decrees. However, the use of Federal troops to bring about compliance with Federal court desegregation orders has been and will continue to be the exception rather than the rule.

Consequently, the real danger ahead, in my view, is not increased forcible resistance to desegregation, but a widespread acceptance of a new compromise of those rights now guaranteed even American Negroes by the Supreme Court's decisions barring state-enforced racial segregation in public schools. We are in danger of having imposed upon us, in place of full and complete implementation of the 1954 decision, "tokenism" as the successor to "separate but equal." This is a real danger because the so-called moderates, both North and South, have accepted "tokenism," or the admission of a few Negro students to previously all white schools, as compliance with the 1954 decision. . . .

Before the protest demonstrations commenced on a wide scale in 1963, we were in grave danger of having "tokenism" substituted for "separate but equal" because of the reluctance on the part of Negroes themselves to move into previously all white educational institutions, to sit at desegregated lunch counters, to ride on the front of the bus, and to take advantage of previously all-white recreational and other facilities. But fear on the part of Negroes to press locally for full and complete equality and implementation of the many court decisions barring segregation and exclusion of Negroes suddenly and inexplicably vanished in 1963. As a result, the emergence of "tokenism" as the progeny of the decision in the *School Segregation* cases is now foredoomed. As President Kennedy said . . . [on June 11, 1963] when he sent to the Congress a proposed new Civil Rights Bill of 1875: "A rising tide of discontent . . . threatens the public safety. . . . The events in Birmingham and elsewhere have so increased the cries for equality that no city or state or legislative body can prudently choose to ignore them." [See "A Moral Issue," excerpts from the Kennedy speech, this section, below.]. . .

If Congress should reenact the Civil Rights Act of 1875 as now proposed, a necessary change in the law shall have been effected. Negroes will once more be required to resort to the courts in some instances to enforce their newly established rights but, of course, in many cases, the change as dictated by law will be voluntarily complied with. . . .

When the Civil Rights Act of 1875 is reenacted, the legislative design for equal rights for Negro citizens of the Reconstruction Congress shall have been completed. Then, as Charles Sumner said, we shall have erected in law all of the protection necessary to give Negro citizens equal public rights with white citizens.

THE 1964 CIVIL RIGHTS LAW[2]

[The following is a summary of the key provisions of the 1964 Civil Rights Law.]

Title I

VOTING RIGHTS. Outlaws racial discrimination in qualification of voters for Federal elections. Prohibits denial of voting rights in Federal elections because of registration errors "not material" in determining voter qualification. Forbids literacy tests as qualifica-

[2] From "What the New Rights Measure Provides." *National Observer.* p 13. Je. 22, '64. Reprinted by permission.

tion for voting in Federal elections unless such tests are administered in writing to all voters and a copy of the test a voter has taken, and the answers, are provided the voter requesting them within twenty-five days after his request. Provides that literacy "shall be a rebuttable presumption" if a would-be voter has completed the sixth grade in school.

Authorizes the United States Attorney General and a defendant in a voting case to request a three-judge Federal court to hear cases in which the Attorney General seeks a finding that a pattern or practice of discrimination exists. Authorizes appeal from a three-judge court directly to the United States Supreme Court.

Prohibits prosecution more than once (e.g., for both criminal contempt and for violation of the law) for the same act or omission.

Title II

INJUNCTIVE RELIEF AGAINST DISCRIMINATION IN PLACES OF PUBLIC ACCOMODATION. Bars discrimination and segregation in places of public accommodation such as inns, hotels, motels, restaurants, lunch counters, theaters, sports arenas, service stations, and concert halls if interstate commerce is affected. According to this title, interstate commerce is affected if "a substantial portion" of goods sold or exhibited move in interstate commerce or if the accommodations in question are on the premises of an establishment involved in interstate commerce (e.g., a restaurant in a train station). Specifically exempted from this provision are private clubs and rooming houses with no more than five rooms for hire, when the proprietor is a resident.

Makes state and local laws permitting or requiring discrimination or segregation in places of public accommodation covered by this title unenforceable by prohibiting attempts to punish persons who attempt to exercise the right of freedom from segregation and discrimination in public accommodations.

Permits an aggrieved person to seek protection of a Federal court order "whenever any person has engaged or there are reasonable grounds to believe that any person is about to engage" in acts prohibited under this title. Authorizes the court to permit the Attorney General to step in to seek court orders covered by this title.

Prohibits any civil action seeking such court orders and prohibits criminal proceedings for thirty days from the time of complaint in states or communities where the alleged discriminatory practices are prohibited by local law.

Permits the court, in states where alleged discriminatory practices are not covered by local or state law, to defer civil and criminal action for as long as 120 days while the matter is referred to the Community Relations Service established by Title X of this bill, if the court believes there is a possibility of obtaining voluntary compliance with provisions of this title.

Permits the Community Relations Service to conduct closed hearings unless the court, the person filing the complaint, the defendant, and the service agree otherwise.

Permits the Attorney General to move for a temporary or permanent court order against discriminatory practices if he has "reasonable cause" to believe that any person or group is engaged in discriminatory practices covered by this title. Permits the Attorney General to ask for a three-judge Federal court to hear cases covered by this section. This request must be accompanied by a certificate saying the case "is of general public importance." Authorizes appeal from a three-judge court under this section directly to the United States Supreme Court.

Title III

DESEGREGATION OF PUBLIC FACILITIES. Authorizes the Attorney General to file civil suits to end discrimination or segregation in facilities, except schools, owned by state or local governments, upon receipt of complaints by aggrieved persons, if he believes the complaints have merit and the person making the complaints are unable to bear the costs of filing the suits or would be physically endangered or financially hurt by filing such suits.

Title IV

DESEGREGATION OF PUBLIC EDUCATION. Orders the United States commissioner of education to conduct a survey on the effects of discrimination and segregation on equal educational opportunity in public schools and report his findings to Congress and the President within two years from enactment of this title.

Authorizes the commissioner to provide technical assistance, such as advice on special educational problems, to states, school boards, and schools in order to implement desegregation. Authorizes the commissioner to make Federal funds available to facilitate training of teachers and administrators to cope with problems of desegration.

Authorizes the Attorney General, upon receipt of a complaint that an individual has been refused admission to and removed from a public college because of discrimination, or a complaint that a school board has deprived children of equal protection of the laws, to file suit on behalf of that person if the person is unable to bear the costs of the suit or if, in the Attorney General's opinion, the complaining person would be endangered by filing suit.

This title specifically declares that "desegregation shall not mean the assignment of students to public schools in order to overcome racial imbalance."

Title V

COMMISSION ON CIVIL RIGHTS. Provides for at least thirty days' notice of Civil Rights Commission hearings. Empowers the Civil Rights Commission to serve as a national clearinghouse for information on denial of equal protection of the laws due to discrimination in the field including, but not limited to, voting, education, housing, employment, use of public facilities, transportation, and administration of justice.

Title VI

NONDISCRIMINATION IN FEDERALLY ASSISTED PROGRAMS. Bars discrimination in programs assisted by the Federal Government, excluding Federal insurance and guaranty programs. Authorizes the assisting agency to order an end to discrimination in federally assisted projects, with the order becoming effective upon the approval of the President.

Authorizes termination of an assistance program in cases of noncompliance, provided that compliance with the law cannot be obtained by voluntary means. Provides that notice of termination of assistance under this title and all pertinent facts of the case be submitted by the head of the Federal agency involved and to the appropriate committees of the House of Representatives and of the Senate. No termination order would be effective until thirty days from the date the report is submitted to the appropriate congressional committees.

Title VII

EQUAL EMPLOYMENT OPPORTUNITY. Applies to individuals, corporations, associations, partnerships, unincorporated organizations, and labor unions engaged in business affecting interstate commerce. Excludes employers who have less than twenty-five employees, private clubs, the United States Government, and religious organizations.

Provides that this title becomes effective one year from the date of its enactment. Provides that for one year thereafter, businesses having fewer than one hundred employees shall not be covered by this title; for the second year thereafter, businesses having fewer than seventy-five employees shall not be covered; for the fourth year and thereafter, only businesses having fewer than twenty-five employees shall not be covered.

Prohibits discrimination and segregation in hiring practices and in wage practices. Prohibits discrimination in labor union membership. Prohibits discrimination against an employee because the employee has opposed practices prohibited by this title.

Creates an Equal Employment Opportunity Commission to be composed of five members, not more than three of whom shall be from the same political party. Members are to be appointed by the President with the advice and consent of the Senate. Provides for staggered five-year terms for members of the commission. Provides that the President shall appoint the commission's chairman and vice chairman.

Empowers the commission to investigate charges of employment discrimination and "endeavor to eliminate any such alleged unlawful employment practice by informal methods of conference, conciliation, and persuasion." Prohibits the commission from acting for sixty days in states that have fair-employment laws, if a state or local agency is involved in the case.

Empowers the commission to sue for compliance, and authorizes the court to permit intervention in such a suit by the United States Attorney General. Authorizes the Attorney General to sue for compliance, and authorizes the Attorney General to ask for a three-judge Federal court if he certifies the case "is of general public importance." Authorizes appeal from a three-judge court directly to the United States Supreme Court.

Provides that employers covered by the act post notice of fair-employment-practice provisions of the act. Provides that the President, "as soon as feasible after the enactment of this title," convene one or more conferences to acquaint the leaders of groups who may be affected by this title with its provisions.

Title VIII

REGISTRATION AND VOTING STATISTICS. Orders the Secretary of Commerce to compile voting and voter-registration statistics, including age and race data, in areas recommended for survey by the Civil Rights Commission. This is to be done in connection with the 1970 census. Provides that no person may be compelled to disclose his race, national origin, political affiliation, or how he voted.

Title IX

INTERVENTION IN CIVIL RIGHTS CASES. Provides that the Attorney General may intervene in any civil suit for relief from denial of equal protection of the laws due to discrimination if he certifies the case "is of general public importance."

Title X

ESTABLISHMENT OF COMMUNITY RELATIONS SERVICE. Establishes in the Department of Commerce a Community Relations Service, with a director appointed for a four-year term by the President with the advice and consent of the Senate. Empowers the service to provide conciliation assistance to communities and persons involved in discrimination disputes. Provides that the service "shall, whenever possible, in performing its functions, seek and utilize the cooperation of appropriate state or local, public, or private agencies." Provides that the service's conciliation work be confidential and without publicity.

Title XI

Provides for a $1,000 fine or six months' imprisonment for a person found guilty of criminal contempt under Titles II, III, IV, V, VI, or VII of this act. Provides for jury trials under these titles if the defendant so requests.

THE MEANING OF THE CIVIL RIGHTS ACT[3]

By Alexander M. Bickel

[The 1964 Civil Rights Act] is a statutory booklet some 18,000 words long. It is divided into eleven titles or chapters. Title I, on voting, which is in the form of amendments to the Civil Rights Acts of 1957 and 1960, plugs loopholes that have turned up in the course of litigation under those statutes. It applies only to Federal elections, and orders state registrars to use the same standards in qualifying Negro voters as in qualifying whites; it also forbids them to disqualify an individual for minor errors (those which are not really material to his qualifications) in an application to register.

The title then deals in some detail with literacy tests. It provides that they may not be administered to any applicant for registration unless they are administered to all applicants, and that they may be administered only in writing, with a certified copy of the test to be furnished to the individual upon request. Thus the disqualification of Negro Ph.D.'s on grounds of illiteracy becomes more difficult. But the Attorney General may certify that these provisions shall have no effect in states in which he is satisfied that literacy tests are fairly used, so that the kind of quick oral test given in many Northern states is likely to be unaffected. As an additional safeguard, it is then provided that anyone with a sixth-grade education, obtained in any school in which instruction is carried on predominantly in English, is presumed to be sufficiently literate to vote in Federal elections; if a state wishes to disqualify him, it must prove him to be illiterate—which is to say, it must prove to the satisfaction of the Federal courts that its standards of literacy, as applied to such an individual, make sense.

Heretofore, standards of literacy could be attacked only on the ground that they were unequally administered, even if they required the applicant to do such preposterous things as to render a legal opinion on the meaning of any provision of the Mississippi constitution. (It is noteworthy that this new statutory presumption does not touch requirements that literacy be in

[3] From "The Civil Rights Act of 1964," by Alexander M. Bickel, professor of law at Yale University. *Commentary.* 38:33-9. Ag. '64. Reprinted from *Commentary,* by permission; copyright © 1964 by the American Jewish Committee.

English, under which Puerto Rican voters, literate in Spanish only, may be disqualified in New York, for example.)

Finally, this and other titles—by enabling the Attorney General to get voting and other civil rights cases heard by three-judge courts, rather than by single Federal judges—give him the means to circumvent delays and other obstructionist tactics to which he has been subjected by a few segregationist Federal judges in the South. It is unfortunate that such a cumbersome procedure should have had to be imposed on a busy and over-burdened Federal judiciary, and the necessity for it emphasizes the importance of care in the selection of Federal judges in the South.

The Law on Public Accommodations

Title II is the public accommodations title. It defines a public accommodation as any inn, hotel, motel, or other establishment providing lodging to transient guests, excepting only what came to be known in Washington as Mrs. Murphy's boarding house (meaning an establishment which offers no more than five rooms for rent, and in which the owner also lives); any restaurant or other place that sells food for consumption on the premises, including lunch counters in retail stores; any gasoline station; any place of entertainment, including theaters and sports arenas; and any other establishment which is physically located within the premises of one of the places just listed, and which holds itself out as serving the patrons of such a place (this being the provision under which some barber shops, for example, may be included, and some not). A public accommodation, so defined, is subject to this title if "its operations affect commerce, or if discrimination or segregation by it is supported by state action."

Commerce is said to be automatically affected by all the establishments in the hotel category, on the theory that hotels serve transients, most of whom cross a state line or two, and that the movement of persons across state lines is commerce within the sense of the constitutional provision defining the powers of Congress. Establishments in the restaurant category and gasoline stations affect commerce if they serve interstate travelers, or if a substantial portion of the food or gasoline or other products they sell has moved across state lines. Places of entertainment affect commerce if the thing or performers they exhibit have moved across state lines. Discrimination or segregation is "supported by state action," and thus prohibited whether or not the establishment affects commerce, if it is required by a state, formally by statute or informally by official action or pressure.

All these definitions, however, are expressly made inapplicable to a bona fide private club or other establishment not open to the public, except as a club or the like may open some of its facilities to the general public, in which event the title is applicable to those facilities. In establishments covered, the act declares all persons to be entitled to full and equal enjoyment of everything that an establishment offers, without discrimination or segregation on account of race, religion, or national origin. It is unlawful also for any third party to attempt to prevent an establishment from extending the privileges secured by this title to an individual, or to attempt to prevent an individual from claiming his privileges.

Persons aggrieved by a violation of this title may obtain from a Federal court a decree directing that the violation cease. And there is a valuable provision authorizing the courts to appoint an attorney for a complainant in a suit under this title, and to allow him a reasonable attorney's fee as part of the costs awarded to him if he wins. However, if the violation occurred in a state which prohibits discrimination in public accommodations under its own law, complaint must first be made to the state authorities, and there can be no suit in the Federal court until the state authorities have had thirty days to deal with the complaint. Subsequently, the Federal court may stay its own proceedings until the termination of any local proceedings that may have been undertaken. But ultimately, if the complainant is unsatisfied with what the state has been able to do, he retains his essential Federal right to redress.

In a state which has no public accommodations law of its own, the Federal court in which suit has been brought may refer the matter to the Community Relations Service for a total of no more than 120 days, if the court believes that a reasonable possibility exists of securing voluntary compliance. The Service may investigate and hold private hearings. Suits by the Attorney General on behalf of the Government are possible only when he "has reasonable cause to believe that any person or group of persons is engaged in a pattern or practice of resistance."

Title III authorizes the Attorney General to bring suit to desegregate public facilities, other than public schools or colleges, which are owned or operated by or on behalf of any state—parks, golf courses, municipal auditoriums, and the like. Judicial decisions have long since made clear the law as to such facilities, which turns on a constitutional right to equal access, as part of the general right to equal treatment at the hands of all units of government. Hence, the point of this title is merely that the Attorney General is now enabled to bring suit, rather than private parties only.

The Law on Education

Title IV is the education title. It requires the Commissioner of Education, who heads the hundred-year-old Office of Education in the Department of Health, Education and Welfare, to make a survey and report, within two years, on the availability of equal educational opportunities to individuals of all races and religions in public institutions at all levels throughout the country, North and South. It then empowers him to render technical assistance to local authorities in the preparation and implementation of desegregation plans. A national professional agency will thus be in a position to work out and validate methods for dealing with special educational problems arising from desegregation.

The Commissioner is also authorized to arrange and finance institutes for special training for teachers and administrative personnel who have to deal with problems of desegregation. But desegregation is so defined that the Commissioner will be unable to concern himself with what are commonly called problems of racial imbalance; aside from the survey and report, the effect of these provisions will thus be felt mainly in the South, and only, if at all, in such school districts in the North as may be found to have intentionally gerrymandered school attendance areas for purposes of separating the races.

The Attorney General's new authority to litigate school cases is similarly limited. One . . . amendment, moreover, was careful to provide that nothing in the title should be constructed to empower any court to order the achievement of racial balance through the transportation of pupils from one school to another.

Title V extends for four years the life of the Civil Rights Commission, an investigative body established by the act of 1957, which has done some valuable fact-gathering in the past.

Title VI embodies the requirement that there be no discrimination in federally assisted programs (other than those assisted by way of contracts of insurance or guaranty), and empowers the President ultimately to withhold funds as a penalty for noncompliance. The title carries certain procedural safeguards, as it ought.

The Law on Employment

Title VII is headed "Equal Employment Opportunity." It applies to any individual or corporate or other legal entity regularly employing twenty-five or more persons; to employment agencies, including the United States Employment Service and the system of state and local employment services which receive Federal assistance; and to labor unions. Employers and labor unions are covered only if their activities affect interstate commerce. Unlike the public accommodations provisions, this title does not spell out the meaning of the technical phrase, "affect commerce," for its own purposes, but adopts the well-established definition that has been evolved under the Federal labor law, and that covers a very great deal, indeed.

This title makes it unlawful for any employer to fail to hire or to discharge, or otherwise to discriminate, in compensation or other terms of employment, against any individual because of his color, religion, sex, or national origin. Similar prohibitions apply to employment agencies and to labor unions. The latter are also forbidden to cause an employer to discriminate, and apprenticeship and other training programs must be open to all without discrimination. Exemptions are provided for the case where religion, sex, or national origin may be a legitimate occupational qualification. With a view to demands recently voiced by Negro organizations in the North, the title specifically forswears any requirement of preferential treatment for the purpose of curing an imbalance in the racial composition of a given body of employees or apprentices.

Complaints of a violation of this title may be made either by a person aggrieved or by a member of the Federal Equal Employment Opportunity Commission, which the statute establishes. The initial Federal addressee of such complaints is the commission. The commission is to investigate and, without undue publicity, make every attempt to secure compliance with the law. Its visitatorial powers are considerable. It is authorized to examine witnesses under oath and require the production of documentary evidence, and it may seek the aid of Federal courts when it runs up against a recalcitrant witness. It may require employers, labor unions, and employment agencies to keep relevant records and to make periodic reports, and it may cause them to post conspicuous notices on their premises informing all concerned of their rights and privileges under this title. In a state which has a fair employment practices law of its own, the local authorities are given a period of up to 120 days to deal with any complaint, and before that period is up, the Federal commission may not intervene. Elsewhere, Federal jurisdiction attaches immediately.

In either case, if the Federal commission, having investigated and tried persuasion, fails to achieve compliance, an aggrieved individual may bring suit in a Federal court, which is again empowered to appoint a lawyer for him and to award him a lawyer's fee if he wins. The court may not only order the defendant to stop discriminating on pain of contempt of court, but may also give special remedies, such as an order of reinstatement of an employee with back pay. The commission itself has no litigating authority, except that it may initiate civil contempt proceedings when a decree handed down in a private suit has been disobeyed. As under the public accommodations title, the Attorney General is authorized to sue to enforce this title only when he finds that there is "a pattern or practice of resistance."

Those portions of this title which establish the commission and give it its investigatory powers went into effect, like the rest of the act, when the President signed it. But the provisions defining and prohibiting discriminatory practices do not go into effect until a year later. There is that much of a period of grace and adjustment. Moreover, these provisions will become effective in 1965 only for employers of one hundred or more. Another year will pass before they are applicable to employers of seventy-five or more, and they will be fully applicable to all employers covered after yet another year (that is, in 1967).

Of the remaining four titles, one (X) sets up the Community Relations Service; another orders a special census of voters, with a view to the highly remote and, on its merits, highly dubious possibility of applying Section 2 of the Fourteenth Amendment, which would cut down the representation in the Federal House of states that deny the vote to some of their citizens. For the rest, there are some technical provisions, the most important of which, mentioned earlier, deals with jury trials.

The Significance of the Act

Without question, this Civil Rights Act is a momentous statute, comparable in importance to the Interstate Commerce Act of 1887 and the reforms of the first Wilson administration and of the first two administrations of Franklin Roosevelt. In the long view, the significance of such a statute rises quite above this or that inadequacy in its provisions. The point is that it commits the Federal government, and particularly Congress—which can do things neither the President nor the judiciary, despite their prior commitment, could do alone—to a set of national goals that reach beyond minimal constitutional requirements.

The commitment is not likely to be revoked, and the goals are not likely to be reduced. Over the years, an organic enactment like this trails further judicial and legislative law in its wake. There will be interpretations and amendments, all striving to make it, like the Federal union itself, "more perfect." And they will be achieved, despite occasional setbacks, more easily than the initial step. Such a statute affects the expectations and aspirations of the people, and the sense of duty and function of the institutions of government. For everyone concerned, it changes the universe of discourse.

But that is the long view. More immediately, how will the act be translated into everyday life, North and South? Its address is largely to the South. In its education and employment titles, and in some measure even in the voting and Federal assistance titles, it explicitly excludes application to problems that are typically Northern. To be sure, grievances in the North are, by and large, difficult and in the short run often impossible to redress by legislation. They are rooted, on the whole, not in deficiencies in the legal order, or in blatant discriminations that can be dropped with immediately visible results, but in deeply intricate features of the society which can be reorganized only over time.

For all that, however, it is regrettable that the act on its face looks in many places like a regional measure, for this lays it open to the deadly charge that Northerners are mostly interested in dealing with the racial difficulties of others, but not with their own. Even so, the act will not be entirely without effect in the North: it will have some supportive effect on extralegal pressure applied by the Negroes themselves; the public accommodations and employment titles will activate similar laws that have lain in some disuse in many states; and these titles will be widely obeyed in the North, even by people who in the past chose to shut their eyes to the state statutes. Moreover, the Community Relations Service, which is not confined merely to seeking compliance with the mandatory provisions of the act, may prove to be a useful presence in the North, too.

In the South, provided only that the Justice Department is given enough money to double or triple its staff of civil rights lawyers, registration of Negro voters and public school desegregation ought to pick up quite noticeably, even if there is no great movement toward voluntary compliance. Results should be forthcoming within a reasonably short time with respect also to federally financed programs, of which there are a great many, including hospitals, libraries, vocational training, aid to higher education, and more.

The public accommodations and employment titles, affecting as they do the actions not only of officials but of many thousands of private persons and institutions, must, like all such pervasive regulatory measures, gain general acceptance, however grudging, in order to be effective. It will take, said Senator Goldwater [Republican, Arizona], a police state to enforce this law, and he was almost right; it *would* take [see "A Vote Against the Civil Rights Bill," this section below]. Absolute enforcement of any statute that is resisted consistently and on principle by substantial numbers of people would require a police state. But we do not expect absolute enforcement in such circumstances. By means of occasional enforcement, *pour encourager les autres* [in order to encourage others], and by other means of inducement and persuasion, we undertake rather to reduce the number of those who resist. That is what is in prospect in the South for the public accommodations and equal employment titles, and that is why the Equal Employment Opportunity Commission and the Community Relations Service, which are inducing rather than enforcing agencies, are so important.

Of course, inducement, persuasion, and mediation would not be very effective if the law did not declare in mandatory fashion some standard of behavior to which the mediators can urge people to measure up. And persuasion is not unnaturally hampered if an adamant refusal to be moved by it is known to be an alternative that never costs anything. Yet, while enforcement is a sword that is sometimes wielded, its chief uses are Damoclean.

At the beginning, however, litigation will play a role out of proportion to its eventual significance in rendering the public accommodations and equal employment titles effective. For although there will be some voluntary compliance almost immediately, some of it will await the outcome of the first round of litigation. As with all new statutes, there are issues of meaning and application about which doubt is legitimately possible, and which only litigation can authoritatively resolve. We may expect that the constitutionality of the titles dealing with public accommodations, employment, and Federal financial assistance will be attacked at wholesale—the constitutionality of other provisions being for the most part quite specifically settled by existing decisions.

Despite assertions to the contrary, there is no doubt that the public accommodations and employment titles are constitutional on their face and in general application, and that they will be so held by the Supreme Court in very short order. They rest on the power of Congress to regulate interstate commerce, a concept broadly defined in many contexts in the past, some of which—for example, wages-and-hour and child-labor legislation, the Pure Food and Drug Act, labor legislation in general, and the Mann Act—are quite analogous. Nor is there any doubt of the power of the Federal Government to set conditions on the disbursement of Federal funds; indeed, under decided cases, there is considerable doubt whether the Federal Government may constitutionally allow its funds to be used in discriminatory fashion.

Beyond the constitutional issue, there will be questions of construction. Such questions, becoming increasingly marginal, will continue to arise throughout the life of the statute. A number of initial ones can be foreseen. There are sure to crop up in the South things like "intrastate hotels" accepting no interstate travelers, "intrastate theaters" offering only local entertainment, and all varieties of private clubs. Their *bona fides* will be subject to litigation, as will the question, assuming *bona fides,* whether the statute was intended to cover them. In one instance —in the case of restaurants—the statute speaks of a "substantial" connection with interstate commerce. It remains for litigation to determine just exactly what that means, and the concept of a substantial connection may be read into other portions of the statute as well. Again, the Attorney General's authority to sue is limited to cases where he finds a practice or pattern of resistance, under both the public accommodations and the employment titles. What does this phrase mean? What is its geographic coverage? Are statistics a sufficient proof of a pattern of resistance?

Before as well as after the first round of litigation, but particularly after, much will depend on the amount of pressure exerted by Negro communities, and on the effectiveness of the Community Relations Service and the Equal Employment Opportunity Commission. The quality of the President's appointments to those bodies, and the kind of public support he gives them, will be extremely important. The President's first appointment—that of former Governor LeRoy Collins of Florida as head of the Service—and the prominence he gave it, augur well for the future. But in any event, the goals are set and they are set high. They will be attained, sooner or later. This statute was the point of no return.

A MORAL ISSUE [4]

We are confronted primarily with a moral issue. It is as old as the Scriptures and is as clear as the American Constitution. The heart of the question is whether all Americans are to be afforded equal rights and equal opportunities, whether we are going to treat our fellow Americans as we want to be treated.

[4] From an address delivered over radio and television by President John F. Kennedy, June 11, 1963. Text from New York *Times.* p 20. Je. 12, '63.

If an American, because his skin is dark, cannot eat lunch in a restaurant open to the public, if he cannot send his children to the best public school available, if he cannot vote for the public officials who represent him, if, in short, he cannot enjoy the full and free life which all of us want, then who among us would be content to have the color of his skin changed and stand in his place? Who among us would then be content with the counsels of patience and delay?

One hundred years of delay have passed since President Lincoln freed the slaves, yet their heirs, their grandsons, are not fully free. They are not yet freed from the bonds of injustice. They are not yet freed from social and economic oppression, and this nation, for all its hopes and all its boasts, will not be fully free until all its citizens are free.

We preach freedom around the world, and we mean it, and we cherish our freedom here at home. But are we to say to the world, and much more importantly, to each other that this is a land of the free except for the Negroes; that we have no second-class citizens except Negroes, that we have no class or caste system, no ghettos, no master race except with respect to Negroes?

Now the time has come for this nation to fulfill its promises. The events in Birmingham and elsewhere have so increased the cries for equality that no city or state or legislative body can prudently choose to ignore them.

The fires of frustration and discord are burning in every city, North and South, where legal remedies are not at hand. Redress is sought in the streets in demonstrations, parades and protests which create tension and threaten violence, and threaten lives.

We face, therefore, a moral crisis as a country and as a people. It cannot be met by repressive police action. It cannot be left to increased demonstrations in the streets. It cannot be quieted by token moves or talk. It is a time to act in the Congress, in your state and local legislative body, and, above all, in all of our daily lives.

It is not enough to pin the blame on others, to say this is a problem of one section of the country or another, or to deplore it. The fact that we face a great change is at hand, and our task, our obligation, is to make that revolution, that change, peaceful and constructive for all.

Those who do nothing are inviting shame as well as violence. Those who act boldly are recognizing right as well as reality. . . .

I shall ask the Congress of the United States to act, to make a commitment it has not fully made in this century to the proposition that race has no place in American life or law.

The Federal judiciary has upheld that proposition in a series of forthright cases. The Executive Branch has adopted that proposition in the conduct of its affairs, including the employment of Federal personnel, the use of Federal facilities and the sale of federally financed housing.

But there are other necessary measures which only the Congress can provide. . . . The old code of equity law under which we live demands for every wrong a remedy, but in too many communities, in too many parts of the country, wrongs are inflicted on Negro citizens as there are no remedies at law. Unless the Congress acts, their only remedy is the street.

I am, therefore, asking the Congress to enact legislation giving all Americans the right to be served in facilities that are open to the public—hotels, restaurants, theaters, retail stores and similar establishments. This seems to me to be an elementary right. Its denial is an arbitrary indignity that no American in 1963 should have to endure, but many do.

I have recently met with scores of business leaders urging them to take voluntary action to end this discrimination and I have been encouraged by their response. . . . But many are unwilling to act alone, and for this reason, nation-wide legislation is needed if we are to move this problem from the streets to the courts.

I am also asking Congress to authorize the Federal Government to participate more fully in lawsuits designed to end segregation in public education. We have succeeded in persuading many districts to desegregate voluntarily. Dozens have admitted Negroes without violence.

Today a Negro is attending a state-supported institution in every one of our fifty states, but the pace is very slow. Too many Negro children entering segregated grade schools at the time of the Supreme Court's decision nine years ago will enter segregated high schools this fall, having suffered a loss which can never be restored. The lack of an adequate education denies the Negro a chance to get a decent job.

The ordinary implementation of the Supreme Court decision, therefore, cannot be left solely to those who may not have the economic resources to carry the legal action or who may be subject to harassment.

Other features will also be requested, including greater protection for the right to vote. But legislation, I repeat, cannot solve this problem alone. It must be solved in the homes of every American in every community across our country.

In this respect, I want to pay tribute to those citizens North and South who have been working in their communities to make life better for all. They are acting not out of a sense of legal duty but out of a sense of human decency. Like our soldiers and sailors in all parts of the world, they are meeting freedom's challenge on the firing line, and I salute them for their honor and their courage.

My fellow Americans, this is a problem, which faces us all— in every city of the North as well as the South. Today there are Negroes unemployed two or three times as many compared to whites, inadequate in education, moving into the large cities, unable to find work, young people particularly out of work without hope, denied equal rights, denied the opportunity to eat at a restaurant or lunch counter or go to a movie theater, denied the right to a decent education, denied almost today the right to attend a state university even though qualified—it seems to me that these are matters which concern us all, not merely Presidents or congressmen or governors but every citizen of the United States.

This is one country. It has become one country because all of us and all the people who came here had equal chance to develop their talents. We cannot say to 10 per cent of the population that you cannot have that right; that your children can't have the chance to develop whatever talents they have; that the only way that they are going to get their rights is to go into the streets and demonstrate.

I think we owe them and we owe ourselves a better country that that.

Therefore, I am asking for your help in making it easier for us to move ahead and to prove the kind of equality of treatment which we could want ourselves; to give a chance for every child to be educated to the limit of his talents.

As I have said before, not every child has an equal talent or an equal ability or an equal motivation, but they should have the equal right to develop their talent and their ability and their motivation to make something of themselves.

We have a right to expect that the Negro community will be responsible, will uphold the law, but they have a right to expect that the law will be fair; that the Constitution will be color blind, as Justice Harlan said at the turn of the century.

This is what we are talking about and this is a matter which concerns this country and what it stands for, and in meeting it I ask the support of all of our citizens.

AN ACT OF LAWMAKING [5]

My fellow Americans:

I am about to sign into law the Civil Rights Act of 1964. I want to take this occasion to talk to you about what that law means to every American.

One hundred and eighty-eight years ago this week a small band af valiant men began a long struggle for freedom.

They pledged their lives, their fortunes and their sacred honor not only to found a nation but to forge an ideal of freedom, not only for political independence but for personal liberty, not only to eliminate foreign rule but to establish the rule of justice in the affairs of men.

That struggle was a turning point in our history.

Today in far corners of distant continents the ideals of those American patriots still shape the struggles of men who hunger for freedom.

This is a proud triumph. Yet those who founded our country knew that freedom would be secure only if each generation thought to renew and enlarge its meaning.

From the Minutemen at Concord to the soldiers in Vietnam, each generation has been equal to that trust.

Americans of every race and color have worked to build a nation of widening opportunities.

Now, our generation of Americans, has been called to continue the unending search for justice within our own borders.

[5] From an address delivered on radio and television by President Lyndon B. Johnson, July 2, 1964. Text from New York *Times.* p 9. Jl. 3, '64.

We believe that all men are created equal—yet many are denied equal treatment.

We believe that all men have certain unalienable rights—yet many Americans do not enjoy those rights. We believe that all men are entitled to the blessings of liberty—yet millions are being deprived of those blessings, not because of their own failures but because of the color of their skin. The reasons are deeply imbedded in history and tradition and the nature of man. We can understand without rancor or hatred how this all happened. But it cannot continue.

Our Constitution, the foundation of our Republic forbids it. The principles of our freedom forbid it. Morality forbids it. And the law I will sign tonight forbids it. That law is the product of months of the most careful debate and discussion. It was proposed more than one year ago by our late and beloved President, John F. Kennedy. It received the bipartisan support of more than two thirds of the members of both the House and the Senate. An overwhelming majority of Republicans as well as Democrats voted for it.

It has received the thoughtful support of tens of thousands of civic and religious leaders in all parts of this nation, and it is supported by the great majority of the American people.

The purpose of this law is simple. It does not restrict the freedom of any American so long as he respects the rights of others. It does not give special treatment to any citizen. It does say the only limit to a man's hope for happiness and for the future of his children shall be his own ability.

It does say that those who are equal before God shall now also be equal in the polling booths, in the classrooms, in the factories and in hotels and restaurants, and movie theaters, and other places that provide service to the public.

I'm taking steps to implement the law under my constitutional obligation to take care that the laws are faithfully executed.

First, I will send to the Senate my nomination of LeRoy Collins to be Director of the Community Relations Service [see "Free Speech," address by Governor Collins, Section III, below].

Governor Collins will bring the experience of a long career of distinguished public service to the task of helping communities solve problems of human relations through reason and common sense.

Second, I shall appoint an advisory committee of distinguished Americans to assist Governor Collins in his assignment.

Third, I am sending Congress a request for supplemental appropriations to pay for necessary costs of implementing the law and asking for immediate action.

Fourth, already today in a meeting of my Cabinet this afternoon I directed the agencies of this Government to fully discharge the new responsibilities imposed upon them by the law and to do it without delay and to keep me personally informed of their progress.

Fifth, I am asking appropriate officials to meet with representative groups to promote greater understanding of the law and to achieve a spirit of compliance.

We must not approach the observance and enforcement of this law in a vengeful spirit. Its purpose is not to punish. Its purpose is not to divide but to end divisions, divisions which have lasted all too long.

Its purpose is national not regional. Its purpose is to promote a more abiding commitment to freedom, a more constant pursuit of justice and a deeper respect for human dignity.

We will achieve these goals because most Americans are law-abiding citizens who want to do what is right. This is why the Civil Rights Act relies first on voluntary compliance, then on the efforts of local communities and states to secure the rights of citizens.

It provides for the national authority to step in only when others cannot or will not do the job.

This Civil Rights Act is a challenge to all of us to go to work in our communities and our states, in our homes and in our hearts to eliminate the last vestiges of injustice in our beloved country.

So, tonight I urge every public official, every religious leader, every business and professional man, every working man, every housewife—I urge every American to join in this effort to bring justice and hope to all our people and to bring peace to our land.

My fellow citizens, we have come now to a time of testing. We must not fail.

Let us close the springs of racial poison. Let us pray for wise and understanding hearts. Let us lay aside irrelevant differences and make our nation whole.

Let us hasten that day when our unmeasured strength and our unbounded spirit will be free to do the great works ordained to this nation by the just and wise God who is the Father of us all.

A VOTE AGAINST THE CIVIL RIGHTS BILL [6]

There have been few, if any, occasions when the searching of my conscience and the reexamination of my views of our constitutional system have played a greater part in the determination of my vote than they have on this occasion.

I am unalterably opposed to discrimination or segregation on the basis of race, color or creed, or on any other basis; not only my words, but more importantly my actions through the years have repeatedly demonstrated the sincerity of my feeling in this regard.

This is fundamentally a matter of the heart. The problems of discrimination can never be cured by laws alone; but I would be the first to agree that laws can help—laws carefully considered and weighed in an atmosphere of dispassion, in the absence of political demagoguery, and in the light of fundamental constitutional principles.

For example, throughout my twelve years as a member of the Senate Labor and Public Welfare Committee, I have repeatedly offered amendments to bills pertaining to labor that would end discrimination in unions, and repeatedly those amendments have been turned down by the very members of both parties who now so vociferously support the present approach to the solution of our problem. Talk is one thing, action is another, and until the members of this body and the people of this country realize this, there will be no real solution to the problem we face.

To be sure, a calm environment for the consideration of any law dealing with human relationships is not easily attained—emotions run high, political pressures become great, and objectivity is at a premium. Nevertheless, deliberation and calmness are indispensable to success.

It was in this context that I maintained high hopes for this legislation—high hopes that, notwithstanding the glaring defects

[6] From address to the United States Senate, June 18, 1964, by Senator Barry M. Goldwater of Arizona, the 1964 Republican presidential nominee. Text from New York *Times.* p 18. Je. 19, '64.

of the measure as it reached us from the other body and the sledgehammer political tactics which produced it, this legislation, through the actions of what was once considered to be the greatest deliberative body on earth, would emerge in a form both effective for its lofty purposes and acceptable to all freedom-loving people.

It is with great sadness that I realize the nonfulfillment of these high hopes. My hopes were shattered when it became apparent that emotion and political pressure, not persuasion, not common sense, not deliberation, had become the rule of the day and of the processes of this great body. . . .

I realize fully that the Federal Government has a responsibility in the field of civil rights. I supported the civil rights bills which were enacted in 1957 and 1960, and my public utterances during the debates on those measures and since reveal clearly the areas in which I feel that Federal responsibility lies and Federal legislation on this subject can be both effective and appropriate. Many of those areas are encompassed in this bill, and, to that extent, I favor it.

I wish to make myself perfectly clear. The two portions of this bill to which I have constantly and consistently voiced objections, and which are of such overriding significance that they are determinative of my vote on the entire measure, are those which would embark the Federal Government on a regulatory course of action with regard to private enterprise in the area of so-called "public accommodations" and in the area of employment—to be more specific, Titles II and VII of the bill.

The Problem of Constitutionality

I find no constitutional basis for the exercise of Federal regulatory authority in either of these areas; and I believe the attempted usurpation of such power to be a grave threat to the very essence of our basic system of government, namely, that of a constitutional republic in which fifty sovereign states have reserved to themselves and to the people those powers not specifically granted to the central or Federal Government.

If it is the wish of the American people that the Federal Government should be granted the power to regulate in these two areas and in the manner contemplated by this bill, then I say that the Constitution should be so amended by the people as to authorize such action in accordance with the procedures for amending the Constitution, which the great document itself prescribes.

I say further that for this great legislative body to ignore the Constitution and the fundamental concepts of our governmental system is to act in a manner which could ultimately destroy the freedom of all American citizens, including the freedoms of the very persons whose feelings and whose liberties are the major subject of this legislation.

My basic objection to this measure is, therefore, constitutional. But in addition, I would like to point out to my colleagues in the Senate and to the people of America, regardless of their race, color or creed, the implications involved in the enforcement of regulatory legislation of this sort.

To give genuine effect to the prohibitions of this bill will require the creation of a Federal police force of mammoth proportions. It also bids fair to result in the development of an "informer" psychology in great areas of our national life—neighbors spying on neighbors, workers spying on workers, businessmen spying on businessmen, where those who would harass their fellow citizens for selfish and narrow purposes will have ample inducement to do so. These, the Federal police force and an "informer" psychology, are the hallmarks of the police state and landmarks in the destruction of a free society.

I repeat again: I am unalterably opposed to discrimination of any sort and I believe that though the problem is fundamentally one of the heart, some law can help—but not law that embodies features like these, provisions which fly in the face of the Constitution and which require for their effective execution the creation of a police state. And so, because I am unalterably opposed to any threats to our great system of government and the loss of our God-given liberties, I shall vote "no" on this bill.

This vote will be reluctantly cast, because I had hoped to be able to vote "yea" on this measure as I have on the civil rights bills which have preceded it; but I cannot, in good conscience to the oath that I took when assuming office, cast my vote in the affirmative. With the exception of Titles II and VII, I could wholeheartedly support this bill; but with their inclusion, not measurably improved by the compromise version we have been working on, my vote must be "no."

If my vote is misconstrued, let it be, and let me suffer its consequences. Just let me be judged in this by the real concern I have voiced here and not by words that others may speak or by what others may say about what I think.

My concern extends beyond this single legislative moment. My concern extends beyond any single group in our society. My concern is for the entire nation, for the freedom of all who live in it and for all who will be born into it.

It is the general welfare that must be considered now, not just the special appeals for special welfare. This is the time to attend to the liberties of all.

This is my concern. And this is where I stand.

THE SOUTH LOOKS AHEAD [7]

In 1963 some 18 million Negroes have broken through the major barriers that for some two hundred years have separated them from equal participation in American life. Within the foreseeable future the system of segregation will be wiped out.

The acceleration of pace in pursuit of that objective will intrigue historians of the future. The ugly, murderous mob at Oxford, Mississippi, created by the folly of a Mississippi long withdrawn from the American dream and purpose, was a therapeutic event in that it shocked the national conscience. After all, those who had before Oxford remained aloof from decision could not say, "I approve of Ross Barnett and the policies of the White Citizens Councils." The fact that the Government sent troops there to establish and maintain the constitutional rights of one man was reassuring. . . . It remained for Birmingham, Alabama, its police commissioner Bull Connor, the use of police dogs, the arrest of children, the brutal employment of high-pressure fire hoses, and statements callous and coarse, to provide the catalyst, the quickening of will, the resolution to act from the grass roots of the Delta's rich soil and the ghettos of cities and towns, large and small.

So it was that by mid-summer [1963], one could look ahead and see that New South—about which so many prophets have

[7] From an article by Ralph McGill, editor and publisher of the Atlanta *Constitution*. *Ebony*. 28:99-102. S. '63. Reprinted by permission.

written and prophesied—coming over the horizon. There have been, of course, many new Souths in the long history of that region. But this one of freedom from the expensive and spiritually distorting bonds of a segregated system will be one really new . . . and the first one of truly free and great expectations.

But one could also look ahead and see that there was, and is, a vast need of coordination of all agencies involved in the drive for full citizenship and a broadening of the base. This is not merely a movement of Negro citizens. It involves all those who are committed to the national principles, to all that is meant by the phrase "Western civilization," to the meaning and strength of the Jewish and Christian ethics, and to all those sensitive to the human condition generally.

Such cooperation is of a first priority. There must be well thought out plans for what comes after the ending of segregated practices. (That these will hang on for a time in isolated rural pockets is a melancholy expectation, but not really important to the major need.) It is well understood today that lack of guidelines after emancipation and the end of slavery and the Civil War was disastrous. A hastily conceived reconstruction was concerned with immediacy, and not with the future. A new society might have been slowly and patiently constructed. But there were no plans to educate, to train, to communicate ideas or a philosophy of democratic development. Had there been, then and there, a blueprint something along the lines of the Marshall Plan that rehabilitated Europe politically and economically after the Second World War, the nation would have been spared much painful travail, and an accompanying human and economic loss. There was none. . . .

After Birmingham, in the spring of 1963, had everywhere lighted a grass roots fire in America, the organizations at work in the field of human rights began to feel more sharply than before the need for coordination. It all had seemed to happen so quickly, (though, actually, it did not), that no over-all plan of strategy or tactics existed. The Congress of Racial Equality (CORE), the Students Nonviolent Coordinating Committee [SNCC], the Urban League, the NAACP, and individuals, led by Martin Luther King, had unity of objective. Yet, the more mature knew that even though civil rights were won after a long, hard fight, this, too, would be but a step. There would still be need for implementation. There were others who knew that because of the long isolation of the Negro from American life, a cultural and educational lag existed which would make it difficult for many Negroes—especially those in the rural South and those who had gone from it, untaught and unskilled, to the industrial cities of the East and West—to take advantage of the rights attained.

There were knowledgeable persons who were aware that for many Negroes in the North, jobs were of more immediate emotional appeal than civil rights. A poor, unemployed Negro can see that discriminations lie more heavily on him than on a skilled Negro wage-earner of the middle class or a successful professional man. In fact, the poorer Negro can look about him and see a certain economic kinship, at least, with the long-jobless white man, who, more often than not, is a product of the segregated educational system that has cheated both. The organizations and those who spoke for them soon were commonly agreed on the need for coordination.

As one looks ahead, the NAACP comes strongly into focus. The direct action groups were invaluable. They worked in fields where, often, there was no "law." The student pickets and sit-ins, the Freedom Riders, and all those engaged in eyeball-to-eyeball confrontation with discrimination, telescoped time. They achieved in a relatively brief time what lawsuits could not have won in years. But the NAACP always was, as the legal arm, the great rock in a weary land. It is the organization that must bear the major burden of the future. The attainment of civil rights is not really the major objective. Once these rights are secured, then will come the exacting and demanding task of somehow closing the gulf in education and training, jobs and housing. Talents, skills and abilities unavailable to the nation because of segregation will be released for use in other fields of the nation's politically and economically complex life. The competitive erosion of that release will present many new problems, some as psychologically frustrating as those of a segregated society.

Ironically, as one peers toward the unfolding future, one sees that since only 18 million of the roughly 185 million Americans are Negro, it will be the white population—more especially that of the South, that will benefit most of all. . . .

Political Change

There are signs of a developing two-party system, and of Democrats who do not approve of the racist views of senators and congressmen whose long political life and power in congressional committees have depended on the one-party politics of the region. President Kennedy was continually harassed and denied by this sort of control of the Rules Committee in the House, and by other committees controlled by Southern Democrats who were subservient to the extremist groups in their constituencies.

Most of the pragmatic business of looking ahead in the South fell to the white Southerner. As the Negro's image of himself changed, the image of the region inevitably took on a different aspect. This reached deep into the rural regions. Almost overnight the Negro farm tenant, cropper, or small land owner, seemed to be (and was) "different." He was not, as some said, a new Negro. But in the new climate of things he could publicly say and express thoughts and feelings long suppressed. One month, for example, the Mississippi planters and mayors of cities in that state could, and did, speak of contented Negroes who were being disturbed by outsiders. The next month many of these same Negroes were in the demonstration of discontent in Jackson, the state's capital. It is factual to say that in the rural South the white man was certainly astonished, bewildered, and usually resentful of this change. The trumpets of a new era had blown down the walls of the old Jericho. It was less easy for the rural Southerner to look ahead. His whole economy and society was based on the old ways. But, change being relentless, this Southerner had to look forward, and even if he closed his eyes against what he saw, he nonetheless had to open them now and then.

In the urban areas, and the South is largely urban, there was looking forward. It needs to be said that well before the pickets and the sit-ins there were some few industries and businesses which had looked ahead and begun to upgrade Negro employees and to hire more than before. By 1960 this number had increased, though, comparatively, it was small. By 1963, most of the large corporations and businesses had begun—or had plans ready to put into operation—to upgrade Negro employees who were ready for promotion, and to send others to training schools. Looking ahead, one could see a steady, accelerated improvement in job opportunities for Negroes.

In looking ahead, Negro and white began to understand they had to look back at the low quality of most of Southern education and admit that a segregated system, in a region lacking the income to pay for one good system, had penalized all children with an inadequate dual set-up. The penalty, to be sure, was heaviest on the Negro children, particularly those in the poorer rural areas. Many of those who came from the tenant cabins and the small farms were, therefore, neither prepared psychologically nor technically, for an industrial society. But they were there—and more were coming. This made looking ahead by the white leadership even more imperative.

Looking ahead one may see that it is in the field of voting rights that the real revolution will come. Voting strength will quickly win better schools, will end discrimination in relief benefits, jobs, housing and other aspects of life. The South, free of its burdens of taxes wasted in supporting two systems, and maintaining all the other financially and morally costly trappings of a segregated society, should become the great boom area. The South has sacrificed its children, colored and white, to inferior education, and has, across a hundred years, discriminated, in one degree or another, against all its people. A free South will be, in fact, a New South. The human condition always has had at least three yearnings . . . to be treated as a human being, to have an equal, fair chance to win respect and advancement as an individual in the economic environment, and freely to seek spiritual and cultural happiness.

All this means that attainment of civil rights is only a means to the more distant end—the long-term harvest of social, political, and economic reforms made possible by the possession and use of those rights.

Planning and foresight, which will enlist all Americans, of whatever racial background, to build a stronger nation of commitment and belief is the opportunity offered by the days and nights that move toward us. If we miss this second opportunity—one hundred years after the first—it is unlikely we will have another.

MORE THAN LAW IS NEEDED [8]

The first returns on the effectiveness of the Civil Rights Act of 1964 are in. They are, to be sure, incomplete and early. The titles on voting, education and federally assisted programs call for a great deal of administrative activity, and we know nothing yet of their operation. The employment title provides for a year's period of grace before it becomes binding on anyone. But the sections requiring equal treatment in public accommodations address explicit and immediate commands to the general public, and there is evidence that they have been obeyed—more widely, initially, at least, than some had dared hope.

Many restaurants and hotels have been voluntarily desegregated, including a number in such places as Jackson, Miss., and Birmingham, Ala., and most high officials in the South—with the exceptions of Governor Wallace of Alabama and Governor Johnson of Mississippi—have urged compliance with the law, or have, at any rate, not advocated defiance. Particularly good statements came from Senators Russell of Georgia [Democrat] and Ellender of Louisiana [Democrat], and something of a counsel of moderation and acquiescence was heard even from Senator Strom Thurmond of South Carolina [Republican, former Democrat]. In some measures, no doubt, this heartening initial response is the result of President Johnson's vibrant appeal to the country, and more particularly to his fellow Southerners, at the signing ceremony, and of the promptness with which he set in motion the administrative machinery for the implementation of the entire statute.

All this must not delude us into thinking, however, that the public-accommodations title (let alone the rest of the act) is now effective, and that the problem is solved. It is an all-too-common delusion with us that the way to solve a problem is to pass a law about it and then forget it, and we are naturally prone to seize on facts that seem to confirm what we wish to believe. But the evidence so far is not conclusive. . . .

There is some basis for feeling sanguine, no doubt. And yet a good initial response is not infrequently achieved by laws whose implementation later gives rise to many difficulties. It

[8] Reprint of "Much More than Law Is Needed," by Alexander M. Bickel, professor of law, Yale University. New York *Times Magazine.* p 7+. Ag. 9, '64. © 1964 by The New York Times Company. Reprinted by permission.

seemed for a short while, immediately after enactment of the Eighteenth Amendment, that prohibition would prove effective— so the Wickersham Commission reported ruefully a decade later. And, for the first two years or so, there was a good deal of voluntary compliance with the Supreme Court's school desegregation decision of 1954. In both instances, of course, there was plenty of trouble later.

Voluntary compliance may loom large at first because there are always people who have been waiting—out of timidity or inertia—for the law to nudge them into doing what they have really considered the right and profitable thing to do all along. The forces of resistance, on the other hand, need time to cohere and to encourage themselves.

It is noteworthy in this connection that some good missionary work by the Department of Justice and others during the last year succeeded in obtaining considerable desegregation even before there was a law to comply with. Mostly it was chain organizations, and establishments in metropolitan areas, that agreed to desegregate. This has, by and large, continued to be the pattern. It remains to be seen what happens in hard-core areas, and how much of the desegregation is genuine, rather than a token show.

These caveats are not meant to suggest that the public-accommodations title and other portions of the Civil Rights Act are likely to fail, or that they can work, as Mr. Goldwater said in the Senate, only if we institute a police state. The point is that the act is likely—it is virtually bound—to fail if we take the fatuous assumption that it is bound to succeed.

Laws are not always effective simply because they are there, and because violators are subject to suit. To think so is to forget what the late Roscoe Pound almost fifty years ago called "the limits of effective legal action," to forget that only in a certain kind of social and political situation is law self-executing through its own institutions, and that there are times when extralegal resources must be brought to the aid of the law in order to make it attain its end. Enactment and enforcement of law are sometimes only episodes, even if the single most important and influential ones, in a long and varied process by which society, working through a number of institutions, manages to realize a given purpose. . . .

The limits of law are the limits of enforcement, and the limits of enforcement are the conditions of a free society—perhaps, indeed, the limits of government altogether. If substantial portions of the statute book had to be enforced by direct action, whether through civil or criminal litigation, against large numbers of people, we would have a very different and infinitely more disagreeable society than we do.

To be sure, there is always a residuum of the antisocial, whose numbers the enforcement process, most often the criminal process, strives to reduce, although never with absolute success. And there may be laws, such as narcotics statutes, which some people may be simply incapable of obeying. Still laws about killing and stealing, about the payment of taxes, about contracts, about torts, labor relations—even traffic laws—are effectively, if never absolutely, in force. And yet we have a free society, not a police state.

We invest relatively limited resources in the effort to enforce law, and we sacrifice relatively little of other values in the process. The well-known secret of this operation is that most people, most of the time, need only to be made aware of the law in order to obey it. Much litigation is the consequence of differences of opinion about what the law is or ought to be, not of failure to obey what is clearly the law.

In a simple system, when, as Pound pointed out,

men demand little of law and enforcement of law is but enforcement of the ethical minimum necessary for the orderly conduct of the society, enforcement of law involves few difficulties. All but the inevitable antisocial residuum can understand the simple program and obvious purposes of such a legal system. . . . On the other hand, when men demand much of law, when they seek to devolve upon it the whole burden of social control, when they seek to make it do the work of the home and of the church, enforcement of law comes to involve many difficulties. . . . The purposes of the legal order are [then] not all upon the surface and it may be that many whose nature is by no means antisocial are out of accord with some or even with many of these purposes.

It is then, Pound added, that "we begin to hear complaints that laws are not enforced and the forgotten problem of the limitations upon effective legal action once more becomes acute."

When people in the millions—or even hundreds of thousands —are opposed, intensely, consistently and on principle, to a law bearing directly on their conduct of ordinary affairs, effective enforcement is possible, if at all, only through military occupation. Effective enforcement in the face of determined and widespread opposition is possible, this is to say, only if the private conduct that is to be regulated is subject to more or less continuous official scrutiny, and to more or less continuous coercion. It makes no difference, with regard to the enforcement problem, that the opposition is nationally a minority. As Walter Lippmann remarked in 1926, writing about Prohibition: "When the object is to regulate personal habit and social custom, the majority which matters is the majority of the community concerned."

People in the sort of numbers we are talking about will, of course, control some state governments and many other local authorities, and these in turn may decline to cooperate in the enforcement of a locally unpopular Federal law. But the chief source of the difficulty is not that the Federal Government lacks the basic police power and is helpless without the cooperation of the states. The heart of the matter is that no normal police and prosecuting activity can be effective in such circumstances. Nothing short of the pervasive presence of armed men will do.

As a temporary measure, in case of a breakdown of elementary public order, this has proved necessary in the past, may again be necessary on future occasions, and is well within the authority and capability of the Federal Government. But as a regular and more or less permanent device, it is something from which we recoil, deeming it destructive of the values of a free society, and in the end, quite possibly, ineffective even in terms of its immediate aim.

The true alternatives, therefore, are reducing the opposition by a process of inducement and persuasion, or abandoning the law. Abandonment of the law is not inconsistent with occasional enforcement in specific circumstances. And abandonment does not have to be formal, at least not immediately. The law may stay on the books for a while; it may even be observed in some parts of the country, but if it is substantially abandoned in practice, that ultimately is what really matters. Noncompliance is contagious, and the statute book will conform to the practice.

Most laws—very nearly all laws—it need hardly be repeated, are readily accorded general acquiescence, and are easily effective. But that the alternatives otherwise are as I have stated them, that there are times when law does not gain general consent merely by virtue of having been authoritatively pronounced, and that lacking such consent it cannot be effective—this is demonstrated by antigambling statutes, which coexist with widespread gambling, and by laws regulating common sexual practices, which lie largely in disuse. Further, dramatic proof of the proposition may be drawn from two notorious experiences in American history.

The Fugitive Slave Act of 1850 was enacted as part of that year's broad compromise on the slavery problem, engineered by Henry Clay and seconded by Webster in his famous 7th of March speech. The act had firm support in the Constitution, but it was repugnant to much of the North. Emerson, no wild abolitionist, called it "this filthy enactment," and wrote in his journal: "I will not obey it, by God!" Others, like Theodore Parker of Boston, agitated against it publicly and fiercely. William R. Day, a boy in Ravenna, Ohio, in the eighteen fifties, later a justice of the Supreme Court of the United States, remembered to the end of his days the heated meetings and resolutions against the act, and retained a sense of the limits of Federal law. Many Northern states passed "personal liberty laws," as they were called, which were inconsistent with the act and were really thinly veiled attempts to nullify it. Efforts to enforce the Fugitive Slave Act were often resisted by mobs, were in any event not significant, and soon pretty well ceased. The end result was a hardening and broadening of Northern antislavery sentiment.

Nearly three quarters of a century later, Prohibition was imposed on the country by constitutional amendment. The amendment was proposed by the necessary two-thirds vote of Congress, and was ratified by the legislatures of ten more states than necessary, forty-six in all.

There was some thought that the amendment might, paradoxically, itself be unconstitutional, and the matter was carried to the Supreme Court by distinguished counsel, but the Court held otherwise. In some states, Prohibition was effective, and almost everywhere it abolished the old-fashioned saloon. But in many areas, and signally throughout the urban United States, enforcement soon became meaningless. Large numbers of people discovered, if they had ever thought about it before, that they did not really want Prohibition. The Volstead Act was, of course, openly disdained. Perfectly respectable and substantial people advised violation of it, and public officials condoned violation, to say the least. By the middle of the decade, when repeal did not yet seem a realistic possibility, leaders of opinion talked of nullification in one form or another.

"Conscience and public opinion," wrote Arthur T. Hadley, president emeritus of Yale, in 1925, "enforce the laws; the police suppress the exceptions." In this instance, conscience and public opinion opposed the law, and the exceptions were the rule. Hence no enforcement was possible; the law was no law. When, under President Hoover, an effort was made to achieve more widespread and efficient enforcement, the only result was that sufficient steam was finally generated for actual repeal.

What do these ominous lessons from history teach about the prospects for realization of the aims of the Civil Rights Act of 1964? It is first to be remarked that the Fugitive Slave Act *was* an immoral law, and that the Eighteenth Amendment attempted to regulate conduct that is morally neutral, and as to which one's neighbor or a majority of one's countrymen ought, of right, to have no power to impose their views. The Civil Rights Act of 1964 is a very different affair.

Now, such judgments are not to be escaped. They are decisive, and if by any chance the Civil Rights Act cannot validly be distinguished in this fashion from the Fugitive Slave Law and the Prohibition Amendment, then it may meet their fate. That is the blunt truth, and we may as well be aware of it. If, on the other hand, as so many believe, the Civil Rights Act is a just law, embodying minimal moral requirements that a national majority may properly attempt to impose on everyone, then what the earlier experiences teach is that the country now faces a task of persuasion and inducement, a task of political and social leadership and education.

Pronouncement of the law is the first step, and in itself an important persuasive and educational action. It must be followed not merely by a concerted campaign to convince everyone of the morality and justice of the law, but also by an effort to bring home to the minority the intensity with which by far the greater number of their fellow citizens hold to the law. This will appeal to the minority's interest, which goes beyond the immediate issue, in conforming to the wishes of a national majority, with which, we may assume, they desire to continue in mutual profit to form part of a single body politic.

The crucial point is that there is in prospect a contest of wills. We must not think that it was resolved in Congress and is now behind us. The preponderant majority and the resistant minority remain, in the phrase that was so popular in the Kennedy Administration at the time of the Cuban missile crisis, eyeball to eyeball, and if the majority relaxes, in a failure of patience or in discontinuity of purpose, as it did after Reconstruction, or if it thinks it can devolve its responsibility on some enforcement officials in Washington and forget about it, as it largely did during Reconstruction, the law is from that moment moribund.

A normal rate of enforcement is part of the process of persuasion and inducement. Litigation, even if its other consequences are not overly onerous, is at the least expensive, and the possibility of it will deter in some measure, since although not nearly everyone can be sued, no one knows who may be. But other means of pressure and inducement must also be employed, by the Government and by private groups and interests favoring the law. The inducement of compliance with this law must be a consideration at every one of the countless points at which the activities of the Federal Government—both the civil and military establishments—touch on the private sector and constitute an actual or potential source of benefits. Private entities—not only Negro organizations but all who would like to see this statute rendered fully effective—have an obligation to exert economic, social and moral pressure, and to set an unwavering example. If it is understood that the triumphant passage of this civil rights statute launched a great reforming enterprise, to be carried on by the society as a whole and not merely by the enforcing arm of the Federal Government, then there is every probability of success.

THE LAW AND MISSISSIPPI [9]

There was a time, only a few years back, when the civil rights movement in the South was largely a Christian crusade and Martin Luther King its prophet. Nonviolent protest was seen as a device for producing a "moral confrontation" between the races. Such a confrontation, the early leadership believed, would lead

[9] From "Mississippi: From Conversion to Coercion," by Christopher Jencks, a contributing editor of the New Republic. The New Republic. 151:17-21. Ag. 22, '64. Reprinted by permission.

to a "crisis of conscience" in the white South, which could only end in the white supremacists' accepting their black brothers as equals (or even as moral teachers).

This "conversion strategy" failed—although not everyone perceived its failure immediately and some clerics in the movement (occasionally including King) still talk as if it could eventually work. But by the time the civil rights movement entered Mississippi in 1961, the "conversion strategy" was becoming a minority faith. The movement was going secular, and the assault on Mississippi was led by Robert Moses, a former Harvard graduate student, and the Student Nonviolent Coordinating Committee [SNCC], not by Dr. King or the Southern Christian Leadership Conference.

The movement had begun to evolve what might be called a strategy of limited coercion. The new strategy still relied heavily on nonviolence and direct action, and it was supported by many who still talked about religion and morality. But the hope was no longer to win over the white supremacists to brotherly love; it was to make life so unpleasant for them that they would find compromise easier than massive resistance. Boycotts would hurt white business, demonstrations would cut into tourism. Perhaps more important, Negro protest of all kinds would provoke the white community into violent retaliation, and this would make it easier to pass Federal civil rights legislation and harder for the offending community to attract Northern investors.

The "limited coercion" strategy worked fairly well in some parts of the "new" South, where the business community has become influential and a middle-class distaste for disorder and violence is pervasive. When the demonstrators forced such communities to choose between brutal repression and modest reforms, some chose reform. But Mississippi proved to be still part of the "old," unreconstructed South. Most Mississippians care more for preserving white supremacy than for profits, lawfulness, or other symbols of "progress." In such a setting demonstrations were useful only to build interest among local Negroes and to show the North that the right to vote was still not honored in Mississippi. Soon after entering the state, SNCC leaders began to realize that ending white supremacy in Mississippi would ultimately require the use of force.

This was not an easy thing for people committed to non-violence to believe, nor is it easy for white Northerners to believe today. Over and over we have been told that eventually the Southern white "moderates" would speak out and take control from the "extremists," that the "younger generation" of whites would have different views from the older, that industrialization and prosperity would eventually change Mississippi's outlook, or that some other "evolutionary" force would save the day. An outsider cannot judge such matters confidently, but I can report that very few of those with whom I talked . . . in Mississippi, black or white, had much faith in any of these accommodating influences. Listening to them it seemed to me that if Mississippi were left to its own devices, racial conflict would steadily increase. . . .

But while white violence against Negroes will probably continue, and may evoke more sporadic counterviolence than in the past, an organized upheaval seems unlikely. Negroes in New York, like Malcolm X and Jesse Gray, talk about giving bloodshed a purpose by resorting to guerrilla tactics in Mississippi. Most Negroes on the scene know that such a venture, while appealing to some frustrated young adolescents in Mississippi's few miniature Harlems, could only end in disaster. Mississippi is not South Africa. Its black inhabitants are less numerous than its white ones, and they live on a largely white continent where outside sympathy or help would be unlikely once they started shooting. . . .

Yet if Mississippi Negroes cannot hope to employ force successfully themselves, they can hope to play their cards cleverly enough so that the Federal Government will do their job for them. The present strategy of the civil rights movement in Mississippi rests on this hope. . . .

Northern whites often find this kind of pressure on Washington irritating or puzzling. They feel the Negroes got as much as they had any right to hope for in the new Civil Rights Act, and they feel that "the problem is now one for the courts." This feeling is understandable, for it is based on the notion, widely disseminated by civil rights organizations in the past, that "the problem" is primarily one of segregation and discrimination. This may be true in some places. It is not true in Mississippi. . . .

Is the Law Relevant?

The fact is that the new civil rights law, even if rigorously
enforced, would do little for the overwhelming majority of Mississippi Negroes. The act is relevant largely to the Negro middle
classes, a mere handful of whom are allowed to exist in Mississippi. The midde classes are the ones who can afford to eat in
hitherto white restaurants and stay in hitherto white hotels.
They are the ones whose children will be emotionally and in-
tellectually prepared to profit from white middle-class teachers,
and who will not have to drop out of school to work in the fields.
They are the ones who will qualify for better jobs if and when
discriminatory hiring is abandoned. It will mostly be they who
will pass the voter registration tests if and when these are fairly
administered.

The lives of most Mississippi Negroes, however, will remain
unchanged, and they mostly know it. The act does not speak
either to their poverty or to their fear. Two thirds of Mississippi's
Negro families now have total income from all sources of less
than $2,000. The act will have very little effect on that statistic.
Almost all Mississippi Negro families have at least one bread-
winner who could be fired tomorrow for displeasing a white employer. The act will not change that either. Almost all rural
Negro families subsist on credit from local storekeepers, who can
cut it off at the whim of the white community. The act will not
change that. All Negroes, urban and rural, old and young, exist
on the suffrance of local law enforcement officers, from whose
kindness or brutality the act offers no real appeal. Finally and
most fundamentally, if a Mississippi Negro is to redress his grievances, the United States Constitution requires him to go before
a jury. This jury may not be all white, but it will inevitably
include enough white supremacists to prevent a Negro's obtaining the unanimous vote in his favor which he would need to get
his due from a white man. White supremacy is founded on social
and economic relationships such as these, far more than on mere
segregation or legally-provable discrimination. . . .

A New Politics

What SNCC wants in Mississippi is nothing less than a second effort at Reconstruction, backed by whatever Federal force
and funds are necessary to make the venture successful. . . .

SNCC's basic aim is now a political realignment in the state. First, SNCC hopes the Democratic Administration will repudiate the Mississippi Democratic party, deprive its congressional delegation of party privileges (notably the party seniority which makes them committee chairmen), and refuse to distribute pork and patronage through the present party machinery. A new Northern-style Democratic party would then be organized in the state, with Negroes, labor unions and poor whites as the major shareholders. Conservative plantation owners and industrial managers, as well as small businessmen and die-hard segregationists, would presumably turn to the Republican party.

[In the long run, this prospect depends] on creating a black-white coalition within Mississippi which can win state and local elections. . . . The only way to make a coalition viable would be to increase substantially the number of Negroes registered to vote. In 1960 Negroes made up 42 per cent of Mississippi's inhabitants; if they also constituted 42 per cent of the electorate, enough of Mississippi's white voters could probably be lured to some compromise candidate for him to win state-wide office. This would certainly be true if the candidate had been promised a voice in distributing Federal largess within the state. In many counties Negroes are an absolute majority, and no such coalition would be needed.

In order to make Negroes anything like 42 per cent of the electorate, however, major changes would have to be made in Mississippi's present voting laws. The present laws require, for example, that would-be voters answer, to the satisfaction of white supremacists, questions about the meaning of the state constitution and the duties of a citizen. These questions have no objectively "right" or "wrong" answers, and they invite discrimination by local registrars. Most registrars have accepted the invitation eagerly. The Justice Department has sought an injunction preventing the use of such questions throughout the state, but so far has not obtained it. Even if such an injunction were issued (and there is a good chance that it eventually will be), many literate Negroes would still be reluctant to apply. Black voters would probably not exceed 10 per cent of the total. If the law requiring the publication of would-be voters' names were invalidated, if local registrars were replaced by Federal ones, if the FBI were more energetic in investigating charges of harassment, intimidation and reprisals, and if the Justice Department were more eager to prosecute, perhaps Negro registration might rise to 15 or 20 per cent of the total.

Beyond that, a major revolution would be required. This is true because although there are more Negroes than whites born each year in Mississippi, the combined effect of rural mechanization and employment discrimination forces a substantial fraction of young Negroes to leave the state soon after leaving school. White supremacists welcome the emigration and encourage it where possible. As a result, Negroes constitute only about 34 per cent of all Mississippi adults, and by 1970 the proportion can be expected to drop to 30 per cent.

More important, even a "color-blind" literacy test sharply reduces the proportion of Negroes in the electorate. The new Civil Rights Act says that completion of sixth grade establishes a "presumption" of literacy. But less than half Mississippi's adult Negroes meet this standard, for they began working in the fields when they were ten or eleven. If Mississippi confined voting to those who had completed the sixth grade or passed some equivalent test Negroes would constitute only 21 per cent of the eligible voters. . . .

The only way to raise the proportion of black voters much above 20 per cent in the foreseeable future would be for Congress to establish a huge adult literacy program. And for such a program to reach the mass of Mississippi Negroes, it would have to be administered directly from Washington, rather than working through state or local authorities. Yet direct Federal control goes very much against the congressional temper and is hardly likely. . . .

The probability is . . . that Negroes will not soon constitute more than a fifth of Mississippi's voters. Politically, this means that a liberal Democratic coalition would have to win the allegiance of about 40 per cent of the state's white voters in order to capture state-wide office. At present it is hard to imagine a candidate who could both win support from Negro voters and from 40 per cent of the whites. . . .

Today most Mississippi Negroes still seem to believe in the American dream, if not for themselves then for their children. (At bottom, this goes for most SNCC workers too.) Should they stop believing, as much of Harlem has, should they at long last strike back at white Mississippi, Northern support for their cause would be reduced to a whisper. If the military were to be used at that point it would be for repression, not reconstruction. The only obvious way to avoid such a potential disaster is to give Mississippi Negroes a major voice in their own destinies before they despair, making them part of the Mississippi "power structure." Only the Federal Government has the power to do this; certainly white Mississippians will not do it voluntarily.

What would make the Federal Government move decisively in time? Only killings, I fear. The Neshoba County tragedy [the murder of three civil rights workers] was a beginning, but its effects lasted only a few weeks. It will probably take repeated and dramatic white violence against Negroes to elicit the necessary Federal action. Such violence can hardly be welcomed, but it could at least have therapeutic consequences. If the present situation is simply allowed to deteriorate, and if large-scale black violence against whites eventually begins, it is hard to see how the circle of fear, violence and repression will ever be broken.

LAW ENFORCEMENT AND SOUTHERN COURTS [10]

The United States Supreme Court, speaking with rare unanimity, has declared time and again that the Fourteenth Amendment imposes upon the states a comprehensive requirement of impartiality between the races. It has applied this principle in one context after another—public education, the franchise, travel by common carrier, municipal recreation facilities, privately owned places of public accommodation, and on and on. Yet, in the deep South, acceptance of the principle is still the exception. The most powerful government in the world seems powerless to enforce its laws against local resistance.

The late Earl Long once observed to Leander Perez, the king of Louisiana's Plaquemines Parish: "What are you going to do now, Leander? The Feds have got the A-bomb." Governors Faubus, Barnett, and Wallace have learned that open efforts at nullification are no more effective now than when John C. Calhoun first proposed them. Naked defiance of the Federal law, as

[10] From "Justice with a Southern Accent," by Louis Lusky, professor of law, Columbia University. *Harper's Magazine.* 288:69-77. Mr. '64. Copyright © by Louis Lusky. Reprinted by permission.

at Little Rock, Oxford, and Tuscaloosa, is doomed by its candor. When the prestige and authority of the Federal Government are overtly challenged, there can be no compromise.

But cleverer men, more interested in results than in cheap drama, have devised other defensive weapons, quieter but far more effective. Skilled legal tacticians, they know the weak points of the Federal judicial system and how to take advantage of them. Their rearguard legal operations have been successful enough to cause grave concern. By hamstringing the Federal mechanism for peaceable resolution of divisive issues, they have invited civil disorder and directly jeopardized the openness of our society. Local prejudices have too often been allowed to prevail over the mandates of the United States Supreme Court. And in too many cases, the lower Federal courts have declined to interfere. . . .

Our Constitution allocates to the Federal courts the primary responsibility for enforcing Federal law over local resistance. The need for this enforcement, in fact, was the only reason the Constitutional Convention of 1787 provided for the lower Federal courts—the eighty-nine *district courts,* which are trial courts, and the eleven regional *courts of appeals,* which can review their decisions in most, but not all, cases. The Convention readily saw the need for a supreme court to serve as final arbiter of the Federal law. Two of the South Carolina delegates, however, argued that a supreme court was enough. They favored a system under which the state judges would be obligated to uphold Federal law, with a single Federal tribunal to review their decisions. It was James Madison who argued—properly so—that the Federal trial courts were indispensable for the effective enforcement of locally unpopular Federal law; the Convention yielded to his logic.

The secret of the present Southern resistance lies in canny exploitation of weaknesses in the Federal judiciary as it is now organized and manned. The United States Supreme Court is simply too busy to decide each of the myriad cases arising from local disobedience. It must concentrate upon a relatively few key rulings in which controlling principles can be enunciated, and rely on the lower courts to implement those principles.

The Federal district courts are manned by judges drawn from their localities, a necessity since much of the law they apply is the law of the state where they sit. Being human, these district judges have not remained unaffected by the entrenched social patterns of their communities, of their friends and former colleagues at the bar. These pressures do not affect the Federal court of appeals judges in quite the same way. They serve multistate regions; they are spared the daily contact with the local community which is involved, for example, in jury trials. Ordinarily they act in panels of three or more rather than individually.

"What the district judges need—and what most of them want," political scientist J. W. Peltason has written, "is not the responsibility for making choices, but rigid mandates that compel them to act."

It is therefore the Federal courts of appeals—particularly those for the Fourth and Fifth Judicial Circuits, sitting at Richmond and New Orleans and serving all the states of the Old Confederacy except Tennessee and Arkansas—which can best take the laboring oar in implementing the principle of racial equality. They have performed valiantly. But there are limitations upon the scope of their operations. Unless they are emancipated from these limitations, the constitutional promise will continue to be flagrantly broken. . . .

What the President Can Do

The President of the United States has the power—and the obligation—to appoint judges who, however opposed they may be to integration, however reluctant to go against local mores, will acquiesce in the discipline of the law.

It is absolutely crucial that a President limit his judicial appointments to men who satisfy [the above test]. . . . The President holds the basic initiative. If political pressures prevent him from appointing avowed integrationists, he must surely refrain from choosing men who have made known their distaste for the job the Federal courts are supposed to perform. . . .

The role of the Federal district judge is important because of his vast discretionary authority. Within very broad limits he has the power to decide whether quick provisional relief will be granted, by temporary restraining order or by preliminary injunction. He has the power to expedite or delay a trial. He has the power to decide what evidence goes into the record. He can decide a case quickly, or hold it for months or years. Even the court stenographer, who must transcribe court notes before an appeal can be heard, is subject to his orders on priority of work.

A judge who is willing to abuse his discretionary powers can stultify the law. It is an absolute necessity for President Johnson to appoint district judges who, however they may decide cases, will decide them quickly, facilitate rather than obstruct the appellate process, and, when the higher courts have spoken, enforce their mandates ungrudgingly.

What the Supreme Court Can Do

In declaring the meaning of our basic law in terms consistent with the needs, desires, and aspirations of the people as a whole, the Supreme Court has performed its primary role magnificently. But it has another responsibility: to administer the Federal judicial system in a way that will obtain from the lower courts the full measure of effective law enforcement. The Supreme Court's performance here leaves something to be desired.

Its most notable error was the "deliberate speed" formula, laid down in 1955. The Court had decided the year before, in *Brown v. Board of Education* and a group of similar cases, that public school segregation is a denial of the equal protection of the laws guaranteed by the Fourteenth Amendment. Ordinarily the winning party in a lawsuit gets at least part of what he sued for; if he sues for breach of a contract to buy a house and wins, for instance, the court directly orders the defendant to perform the contract.

But the successful plaintiffs in the school cases did *not* get an order directing their admission to school. What they got was a promise that, at some time in the indefinite future (perhaps after they themselves had finished school), some other Negroes would be given the rights which the Court *said* those plaintiffs had. Coupled with this promise was an admonition to the local school boards to accomplish integration "with all deliberate speed," and a direction to the Federal district courts to ride herd on them. The effect was to shift the responsibility for judicial initiative, in cases demanding drastic change of settled local customs, to the very sector of the Federal judiciary least fit to assume it.

It is time to write off the "deliberate speed" formula as a sad mistake; the Supreme Court, in the spring of 1963, gave some basis for hope that this might be done—serving notice that the conditions which originally led to the adoption of the formula no longer prevail. But this in itself is not enough. The demonstrated need of the Federal district courts for relief from the primary burden of changing local mores must be recognized as a general tenet of judicial administration. A lesson bought so dearly must not be forgotten.

The Supreme Court has further invited evasion of judicial responsibility by the district courts by developing the novel and curious doctrine known as "abstention." Until 1941, the Court had proceeded on the premise that Federal courts are obligated to decide cases within their jurisdiction, even though this involved judging doubtful questions of state law. There had been no departure from the emphatic affirmation of Chief Justice Marshall in 1821:

> With whatever doubts, with whatever difficulties, a case may be attended, we must decide it, if it be brought before us. We have no more right to decline the exercise of jurisdiction which is given, than to usurp that which is not given. The one or the other would be treason to the Constitution.

But in the 1941 *Pullman* case, a very involved Texas public-utility case, the United States Supreme Court under special circumstances directed the Federal district court to abstain temporarily from exercising jurisdiction—which it admittedly had—until the parties in the case had obtained a ruling from the Texas Supreme Court, that is, from a *state* court. Justice Felix Frankfurter, speaking for the United States Supreme Court, tried to make it clear that this abstention on the part of the Federal court would be appropriate only in exceedingly rare cases. But the Pandora's Box had been opened.

In recent years, despite the efforts of the Supreme Court and the Federal courts of appeals to confine the doctrine of abstention to narrow bounds, it has been a continuing temptation to the district courts and has been used widely in racial cases. . . .

Again there is need for Supreme Court action. The abstention doctrine, if retained at all, should be so explicitly circumscribed that no Federal district judge can honorably employ it as a device for avoiding locally unpopular decisions. . . .

What Congress Can Do

(1) The traditional reluctance of the Federal courts to interfere with state *judicial* proceedings, which is based on a vague Federal law on the books in one form or another since 1793, should be severely qualified if not altogether abandoned. The Federal statute derives from the theory, which used to be reasonably safe, that however lawless the political officials of the states may be, the state *judges* will not engage in wholesale defiance of the United States Constitution which they have been sworn to uphold. Elective state judges all over the South have bowed to the general hatred of Federal law on racial discrimination, making no secret of their determination to ignore it. It is a politically profitable position. It won the Alabama governorship for Judge George C. Wallace, and brought promotion from the circuit court to the Mississippi Supreme Court for Tom P. Brady, who had written in his book, *Black Monday:* "The Negroid man, like the modern lizard, evolved not. He did not evolve because of his inherent limitations."

Under such circumstances the presumption of legality which has surrounded Southern state court decisions has become a fiction on racial questions. Congress must affirm the power and duty of the Federal courts to prohibit by injunction *any* state action which frustrates the enjoyment of Federal rights, and to jail *any* state official—even a judge—if he persists in violating the injunction. Many lawyers think this is already the law. But in 1962, in the Mississippi Freedom Rider cases, the Supreme Court declined an opportunity to decide the question, and it may not do so for years.

Confirmation by Congress of this crucial injunction power would provide a solution in the many cases where Negroes are being prosecuted in state courts without any evidence of wrongdoing whatever. The Freedom Rider prosecutions in Jackson in 1961, where 315 people were convicted of breach of the peace solely because they had used the "wrong" waiting rooms in interstate terminals—which they had every right to do—provide a perfect example of this situation.

(2) Often it can be shown that Negroes are unable to get a fair and impartial trial in state courts. In such cases the remedy should be removal from the state to the Federal courts for trial. Congress included this provision in civil-rights legisla-

tion soon after the Civil War, and it is still formally on the books. But in 1879 the Supreme Court, evidently unwilling to believe that Federal rights would systematically be denied in state courts, gave the statute a restrictive interpretation which has deprived it of most of its force. This removal statute should be restored to full vigor without delay.

(3) The process of appeals to higher courts also needs to be changed. On its face, the statute on appeals says that if a Federal district judge refuses to accept jurisdiction of a case removed from a state court, his refusal—which is in legal terms called a "remand order"—cannot be appealed. This means that even if the right to removal were clearly established, it might be frustrated by a weak district judge. The Federal court of appeals—which stands between the district court and the Supreme Court—would be powerless to accept responsibility for the removal of a case. An important case now pending in the courts argues, on the basis of a careful analysis of the legislative history, that the relevant statute does not apply in civil rights cases. But Congress should not wait.

(4) In most cases appeals from the Federal district courts go to the Federal courts of appeals. There is one crucial area of litigation, however, in which the appeal is directly to the United States Supreme Court. If a party seeks to enjoin—to stop the enforcement of—a state statute or local ordinance, as is necessary in many racial cases, then the case is heard not by the usual one-judge district court, but by a specially convened district court composed of three judges. Appeals from the decisions of such courts must go directly to the Supreme Court.

Hence a frightfully busy Supreme Court is deprived of the aid of the Federal courts of appeals. In other cases these intermediate appeals courts perform the important function of keeping the district courts in line with principles announced by the Supreme Court, so that the Supreme Court need not take the time necessary for full review when no unsettled point of law is involved. But a direct appeal from an erroneous decision places the Supreme Court in a genuine dilemma. Either it takes the case, at the cost of time needed for creative decisions on other appeals, or it declines jurisdiction and leaves the district courts, the most conservative sector of the Federal judiciary, with full responsibility.

Appellate review is obviously needed to keep the difficulty of the district judge's task within tolerable limits. But the direct-appeal procedure puts the Supreme Court under great pressure to refuse cases on strained and technical grounds, pressure to which it has sometimes succumbed. Congress should alter this process. Appeals from the decisions of *all* district courts, including three-judge courts, should be sent to the intermediate Federal courts of appeals.

The Real Meaning

Abstract as some of these reforms may seem to the non-lawyer, let there be no mistaking their profound impact on racial matters in the South. The Mississippi Freedom Rider cases, which made yesterday's headlines, have given rise to a complex series of obstructionist legal maneuvers reaching from a municipal court through the lower Federal courts to the United States Supreme Court and back again. They offer a good illustration of the real meaning of the abstention doctrine, the reluctance of Federal district judges to interfere with state court proceedings, the doubts about the right of removing a trial to a Federal court, the apparent unappealability of remand orders, and the general conservatism of Southern district judges.

These cases, which I know well at first hand, went to the courts in May 1961. They show defiance of Federal law in its baldest form—clear legal right opposed by naked power.

All the Freedom Riders did was enter the white waiting rooms at the interstate terminals in Jackson, Mississipi. They were not armed, or profane, or loud, or threatening; they were testing, in an orderly way, their rights. The Federal right at issue was the right to travel unsegregated on common carriers, a relatively peripheral right when compared with education, or employment, or the franchise. The United States Supreme Court had held in a line of cases going back to 1946 that no state could require or permit segregation of interstate or intrastate transportation by railroad, bus, or airline. In 1960 it had *specifically* held that this principle applies to the terminal facilities as well. If the Federal law, which clearly precludes the remotest possibility of successful prosecution under local segregation statutes, could be frustrated in these circumstances, it could be frustrated in just about every case conceivable.

Frustrated it was. In a campaign of attrition a criminal conviction is a valuable thing, simply because getting it reversed takes time, lawyers, and money. The local authorities launched a skillful, exquisitely executed legal operation. The methods they have used—delay and technicality—have since been successfully used in thwarting legal rights in cases all over the South involving schools, voting, and public accommodations.

Some 315 Freedom Rider arrests were made throughout the spring and summer of 1961. Of the 315 defendants, 279 appealed their convictions in Mississippi courts.

It is now *thirty-four months* since the Freedom Rider cases first went to the courts. Because of the delays and the failure of the federal courts to act swiftly and decisively, most of these cases—except those in which the defendants gave up for lack of bail money—have now been processed only through the county court, the next to the lowest step on the judicial ladder.

A few of the convictions have been decided, and affirmed, in the state circuit court. None has yet been decided by the Mississippi Supreme Court. If the Mississippi high court affirms the convictions, the United States Supreme Court will reverse them some time in 1965, barring unforeseen delay. Then the local prosecutor will have to decide whether to set the cases down for retrial and start the whole process over again, if (in accordance with customary practice) the Supreme Court's mandate permits him to do it.

In the Federal courts themselves, the first suit against the Mississippi segregation statutes was filed by the defendants in June 1961. *Twenty-seven months later* the Fifth Circuit Court of Appeals ordered an injunction against future arrests, but did not interfere with the cases still pending in the Mississippi courts. Years could elapse before the United States Supreme Court finally determines the real question: whether Federal courts can and should enjoin obviously groundless state court prosecutions whose purpose is to nullify Federal law.

The estimated outlay required for exercising clearly established Federal rights in entering the white waiting rooms in Jackson has been more than $2,000 (including $1,500 cash bail) for each of the Freedom Riders who appealed his municipal court conviction as high as the state circuit court. The moral damage has been incalculable.

Why It Matters

I wish it were possible for me to say that this anemic judicial performance is a lone aberration. Having begun my career as law clerk to a great Federal judge, I have perhaps even more reverence for Federal judges than do most lawyers. Having engaged in private practice for twenty-five years, I feel the practicing lawyer's normal reluctance to criticize judges. As a law teacher, I must be wary of denigrating the calling which my students are approaching. But the plain fact is that the lower Federal courts are not doing the job for which they were established.

Unless these courts are activated, and soon, the consequences will be serious. Denial of clearly established legal rights violates the pivotal compact of the open society, whose terms are acceptance of present law in return for effective access to the processes of orderly change. Time and again, the Negro has resisted the preachments of separatism and violence. Yet who is to blame him when he feels that litigation has too often been a sham?

But while protection of minorities from invidious discrimination is a large part of the constitutional structure which secures our open society, it is not the whole of it. Individual freedom is many-sided; it must include, within limits, even the freedom to implement wrongheaded and neurotically prejudiced attitudes. The Negroes themselves would suffer, along with the whites, if racial equality had to be purchased at the price of the broader freedom. They are entitled to as good a society as the whites now enjoy—not to a Southern police-state society. Little Rock and Oxford provide no more useful model for the future than does South Africa.

That is why the lower Federal courts are so important. It is up to them to reestablish the rule of law, which has been so severely impaired by the lawlessness of state officials, without depreciating the general freedom of our society. And it is up to the President, the United States Supreme Court, and Congress to provide them with the support they so desperately need to execute their mission.

III. PROTECTING TRADITIONAL RIGHTS

EDITOR'S INTRODUCTION

That the last decade has been a creative period in American political history is shown by the growing respect for, and extension of, our traditional civil liberties. Following World War II and its immediate aftermath, when the Cold War erupted, many of our basic individual liberties were accorded rough-shod treatment in what has become known as the McCarthy Era, after Senator Joseph R. McCarthy, noted for his attacks on government officials and employees as being Communists and subversives.

Largely the reversion to the mainstream of American respect for civil rights is due to the action of the United States Supreme Court under the present Chief Justice, Earl Warren. (See the first section of this compilation.) In a notable series of cases, the rights of free speech, free press, and freedom to travel, and concern for the rights of accused criminals, have been reaffirmed and strengthened.

These gains are dealt with in this section. But one contrary tendency is also noted. It is dealt with by John T. Lynch, a lawyer and former vice president of the Council of International Investigators, in his discussion of possible breaches of the right to privacy brought about by the use of new technological inventions such as electronic transmitters and similar devices. As yet the Supreme Court has not ruled with finality on this question. Whether the use of such devices, either by police officials, or private agents, violates the rights of individuals is not clear, but there can be no doubt that it is a matter of concern to both government and legal authorities.

In the first selection, the specific provisions of the Constitution and its amendments enshrining the traditional constitutional rights are listed and the rights are briefly described. Prepared by a subcommittee of the United States Senate Committee on the Judiciary, this summary is a convenient reminder, even though in such brief compass not all of the nuances of interpretation can be given regarding each provision of the Bill of Rights and the other passages of the Constitution relating to civil rights.

Most of the remaining selections bear out the view that recent Supreme Court decisions have in the main extended the scope of traditional rights.

The speech by LeRoy Collins, former Governor of Florida and now Director of the Community Relations Service established under the 1964 Civil Rights Act, suggests that the right of free speech is coming to be regarded both by individuals and the mass media as a right applying to communications in general. Anthony Lewis, on the freedom of the press, reviews a case in which the New York *Times* was involved. The Supreme Court's decision, which concerned charges of libel, effectively extended the freedom of the press in this case. Likewise the Court has recently extended the freedom of travel concept as indicated by an editorial reprinted from the New York *Times*.

Two articles follow John T. Lynch's discussion of the right to privacy, mentioned above—one by Robert G. Sherrill, a correspondent of the Miami *Herald*, and the other by Senator Robert F. Kennedy, then United States Attorney General. These articles show clearly the concern of the Supreme Court and the Department of Justice for equality of justice before the law— their interest in providing that equal justice, equal rights to legal aid, and equal opportunities for the poor be accorded at all levels of our judicial system.

THE INDIVIDUAL AND HIS RIGHTS [1]

Before anyone can properly understand the scope of constitutional rights, he must realize that we Americans, by reason of our Federal system, live under two governments, rather than one. These two governments—Federal and state—are closely bound together, so that in some matters they function as one; but more frequently their operations are separate and distinct. Within the scope of activity which the people have entrusted to it, each government is master of its own affairs.

[1] From *Layman's Guide to Individual Rights under the United States Constitution*, prepared by the Subcommittee on Constitutional Rights, of the Committee on the Judiciary. United States. Congress. Senate. 87th Congress, 2d session. Supt. of Docs. Washington, D.C. 20025. '62. p 1-12.

Because of the ever-tightening bonds between persons in different parts of the country, there is an increasing interdependence among all Americans. A hundred years ago, the affairs of California were very remote from those of New York; today a jet can fly from Los Angeles to New York in a few hours. Similarly, issues which at one time were considered to affect only persons in one state or one locality may today affect all Americans. In matters concerning more than one state, the Federal Government's authority, when based on powers granted by the Constitution, is supreme. On the other hand, in matters which do not have national implications or as to which the Federal Government has not acted, the power of the state generally remains supreme.

The first ten amendments to the Constitution were adopted shortly after the Constitution had been ratified by the necessary number of states. At that time there was fear that in the absence of specific limitations on its powers, the Federal Government, were it to fall into unscrupulous hands, might infringe upon the liberties of Americans. These original amendments were designed to eliminate this hazard. They are called our Bill of Rights— guarantees of individual liberty. For instance, the Bill of Rights prohibited the Federal Government from ever taking any steps to suppress free speech and freedom of the press, or to establish an official religion.

The Bill of Rights applied directly only to the Federal Government and did not prohibit state governments from taking action that might threaten civil liberty. Until the Fourteenth Amendment was adopted, a state court, insofar as the United States Constitution was concerned, could have found a man guilty without hearing evidence in his defense or without letting him have a lawyer; and a state legislature could have passed laws confiscating the property of its citizens and providing for punishment by torture. Of course, in many states the state constitutions contained provisions which would have prohibited such action; and actually the constitutions of some states contained their own bills of rights before the adoption of the first ten amendments to the United States Constitution. Nonetheless, it is important to remember that the Bill of Rights in the United States Constitution restricts the power of the Federal Government and does not limit the actions of states, cities, counties, or individuals. On the other hand, the Fourteenth Amendment, which is not a part of the Bill of Rights and was adopted many decades later, is applicable only to state action—which for these purposes includes the action of counties, cities, and other sub-divisions of the state.

Whether reference is made to limitations on Federal power or on state power, it deserves to be emphasized that the United States Constitution does not grant a license for individuals to jeopardize the safety and well-being of society. Thus, as Mr. Justice Holmes has pointed out, "Protection of free speech would not protect a man in falsely shouting 'Fire' in a theater and causing a panic." Nor does freedom of speech and press sanction the publication of libel and obscenity. Similarly, rights of free speech and free assembly do not permit one knowingly to en-gage in conspiracies to overthrow by force the Government of the United States. The civil liberties guaranteed each citizen carry with them the obligation to utilize these liberties in such a manner as will not ultimately impair the liberties of others.

Individual Rights and the Constitution

Article I, section 9, clause 2

The Privilege of the Writ of Habeas Corpus shall not be suspended, unless when in Cases of Rebellion or Invasion the public Safety may require it.

This guarantee enables a citizen, subjected to confinement, to petition a Federal court for a writ of habeas corpus, to test whether such restraint on his personal freedom violates the Constitution or laws of the United States. Except in situations where it is impossible for the courts to function, a person may be imprisoned or detained only pursuant to established judicial procedures.

Article I, section 9, clause 3

No Bill of Attainder or ex post facto Law shall be passed.

A bill of attainder is a legislative act which declares someone guilty of a crime and which imposes punishment without a trial in court. An ex post facto law is a law which makes a crime of conduct which was not criminal when it occurred, or which increases punishment for a crime after it is committed. Congress is prohibited from passing either a bill of attainder or an ex post facto law. The Constitution also prohibits a state legislature from taking such action. (See Art. I, sec. 10, clause 1.)

Article III

Article III of the Constitution outlines the structure and power of our Federal court system, the judges of which help maintain the rights of American citizens. Article III, section 2, also contains a guarantee that the trial of all Federal crimes, except cases of impeachment, shall be by jury. The Supreme Court has interpreted this guarantee as containing exceptions for "trials of petty offenses" and certain criminal contempts, cases rightfully tried before court-martial or other military tribunal, and some cases where the defendant has voluntarily relinquished his right to a jury.

This section also requires that a Federal criminal trial be held in Federal court sitting in the state where the crime was committed. Thus, a person is given protection against being tried in some part of the United States far distant from the place where his alleged violation of Federal laws occurred.

Article III, section 3

Treason against the United States, shall consist only in levying war against them, or, in adhering to their Enemies, giving them Aid and Comfort. No Person shall be convicted of Treason unless on the Testimony of two Witnesses to the same overt Act, or on Confession in open Court.

Treason is the only crime defined by the Constitution. The precise description of this offense suggests an awareness by our forefathers of the danger that unpopular views might be branded as traitorous. Recent experience in other countries with prosecutions for conduct loosely labeled "treason" confirms the wisdom of the authors of the Constitution, in expressly stating what constitutes this crime and how it shall be proved.

Article VI, clause 3

Although both Federal and state officers are required to swear or affirm that they will support the Constitution, Article VI provides that "no religious Test shall ever be required as a Qualification to any Office or public Trust under the United States." Thus, a citizen need not fear that his religious affiliation or convictions may bar him from holding office in our country.

The Bill Of Rights

Amendment I

Congress shall make no law respecting an establishment of religion, or prohibiting the free exercise thereof; or abridging the freedom of speech, or of the press; or the right of the people peaceably to assemble, and to petition the Government for a redress of grievances.

Religion

Two express guarantees are given to the individual citizen with respect to his religious freedom. First, neither Congress— nor a state legislature, because of the Fourteenth Amendment— may establish an official church which all Americans must accept and support, or to whose tenets all must subscribe. Secondly, each individual is guaranteed freedom to practice his religion in the manner he chooses. However, this freedom is subject to the restriction that the citizen's religious practices must not conflict with valid government enactments. For example, one may not have two wives and escape conviction for bigamy by attributing his conduct to his religious beliefs. Nor could a person commit an indecent act or engage in immoral conduct and then validly justify his actions on grounds of religious freedom. However, the unpopularity of one's religious beliefs will not impair his constitutional right to worship as he pleases.

By virtue of the First Amendment, as applied to the Federal Government, and the Fourteenth, as applied to state action, the Supreme Court generally has ruled against any governmental assistance to religious causes, even though the assistance may be nondiscriminatory as between different faiths. However, the Court has held that it is permissible for public schools to release students, at their request, from an hour of classwork in order that they may attend their own churches for religious instruction; or for a state to provide free bus transportation to children attending church or parochial schools if transportation was furnished also to children in the public schools. Resolving a conflict between patriotic loyalties and religious convictions, the Supreme Court ultimately determined that it was unconstitutional to exclude children from public schools because of their refusal on religious grounds to salute the American flag. It has also been held by the Supreme Court that these constitutional provisions do not prevent a state from designating Sunday as a day of rest.

Speech and press

As a general rule, a citizen may freely express his opinions orally or in print. The Supreme Court has ruled, however, that this freedom does not extend to the obscene, the profane, the libelous or insulting, utterances which tend to cause an immediate breach of the peace. In many cases where restrictions on freedom of speech have been considered, the Supreme Court has utilized a "clear and present danger" test, whereunder the constitutionality of such restrictions seems to be determined by the probability that, without them, some serious injury to others might immediately and directly result.

Censorship by requirement of official approval or a license in advance for speaking or publishing has been condemned frequently by the courts. While a citizen is free to make speeches on the public streets, he may be prevented from doing so when he uses a loud and raucous amplifier in a hospital zone or when the location chosen for his address is such that it is likely to interfere with the movement of traffic.

Many controversies have arisen about the proper scope of freedom of speech. For instance, Federal employees unsuccessfully attacked in the courts certain restrictions which the Congress had placed on their political activities, contending that they had been deprived of freedom of speech. The Federal Government has won court battles to jail persons who, intending to overthrow the Government, had advocated and advised that such overthrow be accomplished by force and violence and who claimed that their conduct was protected by the right of free speech.

Assembly and petition

American citizens, whether they are meeting for political activity, religious services, or for other purposes, have the right to assemble peaceably. Public authorities cannot impose unreasonable restrictions on such assemblies; but they can impose limitations reasonably designed to prevent fire, hazard to health, or a traffic obstruction. The Supreme Court has emphasized that freedom of assembly is just as fundamental as freedom of speech and press.

The right of petition is designed to enable the citizen to communicate with his Government without obstruction. When a citizen exercises his First Amendment freedom to write or speak to his senator or congressman, he is taking part in "the healthy essence of the democratic process."

Amendment II

A well regulated Militia, being necessary to the security of a free State, the right of the people to keep and bear Arms shall not be infringed.

The Second Amendment provides for the freedom of the citizen to protect himself against both disorder in the community and attack from foreign enemies. This right to bear arms has become much less important in recent decades as well-trained military and police forces have been developed to protect the citizen. No longer does he need to place reliance on having his own weapons available. Furthermore, the Supreme Court has held that the state and Federal Governments may pass laws prohibiting the carrying of concealed weapons, requiring the registration of firearms, and limiting the sale of firearms for other than military uses.

Amendment III

No Soldier shall, in time of peace be quartered in any house, without the consent of the Owner, nor in time of war, but in a manner to be prescribed by law.

Prior to the Revolution, American colonists had frequently been required to provide lodging and food for British soldiers against their will. The Third Amendment prohibited the continuation of this practice.

Amendment IV

The right of the people to be secure in their persons, houses, papers, and effects, against unreasonable searches and seizures, shall not be violated, and no warrants shall issue, but upon probable cause, supported by Oath or affirmation, and particularly describing the place to be searched, and the persons or things to be seized.

In some countries, even today, police officers may invade a citizen's home, seize his property, or arrest him whenever they see fit. In the United States, on the other hand, the Fourth Amendment protects the individual and his property from unreasonable search and seizure by officers of the law. In most instances, a police officer is not allowed to search the home of a private citizen, seize any of his property, or arrest him without first obtaining a court order called a warrant. Before the warrant will be issued to the policeman, he must convince a magistrate that he has "probable cause"—good reason—to believe either that the individual has committed a crime, or that he has in his possession the fruits of the crime or the tools with which he committed the crime.

The courts have ruled that in some instances it is permissible to arrest a man or to conduct a search without a warrant. For example, if a felony is committed in the presence of a police officer, he has the right to arrest the criminal immediately, without waiting to get an arrest warrant; and, if the policeman makes the arrest, he may then search the suspect without a search warrant as well as the immediate area in which the arrest took place. Also in certain instances, a police officer is permitted to search without a warrant vehicles such as automobiles, boats, or airplanes reasonably believed to contain contraband articles. Otherwise, by the time the policeman returned from court with a warrant, the vehicle might be many miles away.

The courts have wrestled frequently with the problem of determining what is required to constitute probable cause for a search or an arrest. Generally speaking the criterion has been one of common sense: Would a reasonable person consider, on the available evidence, that there was a good basis for believing that the person to be arrested had committed a crime, or that the place to be searched contained the tools or fruit of a crime?

Frequently a misunderstanding exists as to what constitutes a search. A policeman has not conducted a search when he overhears a conversation through a closed door, or when, through an open window, he sees a crime being committed.

Evidence secured by means of an unlawful search and seizure cannot be used in either a state or Federal prosecution. Although this rule sometimes permits guilty men to go free, only by forbidding the use in court of evidence obtained by illegal searches and seizures will illegal searches be prevented in the first place.

The Supreme Court ruled that wiretapping—listening in on a telephone conversation by mechanical or electronic means— does not constitute an unreasonable search and seizure. However, Congress has enacted a law which prohibits the use in Federal courts of evidence acquired by such wiretapping.

Amendment V

No person shall be held to answer for a capital, or otherwise infamous crime, unless on a presentment or indictment of a Grand Jury, except in cases arising in the land or naval forces, or in the Militia, when in actual service in time of War or public danger; nor shall any person be subject for the same offense to be twice put in jeopardy of life or limb; nor shall be compelled in any criminal case to be a witness against himself, nor be deprived of life, liberty, or property, without due process of law; nor shall private property be taken for public use, without just compensation.

Grand juries

The Fifth Amendment prohibits trying a defendant in a Federal court for an infamous crime unless he has first been charged with a crime by a grand jury—this charge generally being stated in a bill of indictment. An infamous crime is a felony (a crime for which a sentence of more than one year's imprisonment can be given), or a lesser offense which can be punished by confinement in a penitentiary or at hard labor. An indictment is not required for a trial by court-martial or by other military tribunal. Also, there is no constitutional requirement of grand jury indictment with respect to trials in state courts, but many states have continued the use of grand juries in their criminal proceedings.

Double jeopardy

The Fifth Amendment also guarantees the individual that he will not be tried before a Federal court more than once for the same crime. The Supreme Court has also stated that, under the due process safeguard of the Fourteenth Amendment, state courts may not harass defendants by successive prosecutions for the same offense.

Double jeopardy does not arise when a single act violates both Federal and state laws and the defendant is exposed to prosecution in both Federal and state courts. Nor does a criminal prosecution in either a state or Federal court exempt the defendant from being sued for damages by anyone who is harmed by his criminal act. Furthermore, a defendant may be prosecuted more than once for the same conduct if it involved the commission of more than one crime. For instance, if a person kills three victims at the same time and place, he can be tried separately for each slaying. Likewise, different parts of a single set of acts may violate several Federal statutes. Separate prosecutions for the violation of each statute do not give rise to double jeopardy.

Self-incrimination

The right that every person has not to be compelled in any criminal case to be a witness against himself, signifies that no one is obliged to provide answers to questions tending to convict him of a crime. With certain exceptions, such as in instances where a witness is granted immunity against prosecution, a person need not answer questions in any Federal proceeding which, in light of all the circumstances, tend to incriminate him. By act of Congress, a defendant cannot be called to the witness stand by the United States attorney (who prosecutes in Federal court), and, if he decides not to take the witness stand of his own accord, his silence cannot be commented upon by either the prosecutor or the judge. The courts have not decided whether the Constitution, rather than an act of Congress, permits the defendant to refuse to take the stand and prohibits comment at his silence.

The protection against self-incrimination provided by the Fifth Amendment may be lost by a witness who does not claim it promptly. In fact, the witness must claim the privilege as soon as he is asked a question, the answer to which might tend to incriminate him. Failure to do so may operate as a waiver of this constitutional protection.

Almost every state constitution also contains some safeguard against self-incrimination, although the Supreme Court has not ruled that a state must extend such protection. However, under the due process clause of the Fourteenth Amendment, state and local police officials are prohibited from using coercion—"the third degree"—to extort confessions from persons suspected of crime.

Due process

A due process clause is found in both the Fifth and Fourteenth Amendments as a restraint upon the Federal and state governments, respectively. This clause affords a procedural protection to the end that Federal and state governments are precluded from using unfair methods in law enforcement. For example, were a court to admit in evidence a confession obtained from a defendant by the use of torture, were a court to receive evidence offered against a defendant by a prosecutor who knew such evidence was false, or were a court to presume that a defendant was guilty until proven innocent or to deny him notice of a judicial proceeding and an opportunity to present evidence in support of his contentions, such conduct would plainly violate the due process protection extended by these amendments.

The due process clauses of the Fifth and Fourteenth Amendments also provide other basic protections whereby the state and Federal governments are prevented from adopting arbitrary and unreasonable legislation or other measures which would violate individual rights. Thus, constitutional limitations are imposed on governmental interference with important individual liberties—such as the freedom to enter into contracts, to engage in a lawful occupation, to marry, and to move without unnecessary restraints. Governmental restrictions placed on one's liberties must be reasonable and consistent with due process in order to be valid.

Just compensation

The Fifth Amendment requires that, whenever the Government takes an individual's property, the property acquired must be taken for public use, and the full value thereof paid to the owner. Thus, property cannot be taken by the Federal Government from one person simply to give it to another. However, the Supreme Court has held that it is permissable to take private

120 THE REFERENCE SHELF

property for such purposes as urban renewal, even though ultimately the property taken will be returned to private ownership, since the taking is really for the benefit of the community as a whole. Governmental action which leads to a lower value of privately owned property may constitute a taking and therefore require payment of compensation. Thus, the Supreme Court has held that the disturbance of the egg-laying habits of chickens on a man's poultry farm caused by the noise of low-level flights by military aircraft from a nearby airbase, lessens the value of that farm and that, accordingly, the landowner is entitled to receive compensation equal to his loss.

Amendment VI

In all criminal prosecutions, the accused shall enjoy the right to a speedy and public trial, by an impartial jury of the State and district wherein the crime shall have been committed, which district shall have been previously ascertained by law, and to be informed of the nature and cause of the accusation; to be confronted with the witness against him; to have compulsory process for obtaining witnesses in his favor, and to have the Assistance of Counsel for his defense.

The Sixth Amendment enumerates specific rights guaranteed to the individual who is prosecuted in a Federal court. Many, but not all, of these rights also are available in state criminal trials by virtue of the due process provision of the Fourteenth Amendment. For example, the accused in any Federal criminal case must be provided by the court with a lawyer if he wants, but has been unable to employ, one. In state criminal trials, a similar right exists if the defendant is being tried for an offense punishable by death and in a few other situations when a trial without counsel is considered unfair. The right to counsel in state courts, as granted by the Fourteenth Amendment, is not so broad in scope as that guaranteed in Federal trials by the terms of the Sixth Amendment. [However, see reference to the Gideon case in "Equality Before the Law," this section, below—Ed.]

The Sixth Amendment requires that the accused be brought to trial without unnecessary delay, and that this trial be open to the public. Thus, the members of the accused's family can be at his side during the trial, and newspapermen have the opportunity to cover it. It has already been noted that Article III of the Constitution requires generally that trial be had in the state where the crime was committed. The Sixth Amendment adds the requirement that the trial take place in the district wherein the crime was committed. Therefore, in a state which is divided into two or more Federal court districts, trial must be held in that district wherein the crime is alleged to have taken place.

The jury trial guaranteed by the Sixth Amendment in Federal prosecutions is trial by twelve jurors who must reach their verdict by unanimous decision. This same guarantee is not applicable in a state criminal trial; therefore, states may perhaps abolish the jury trial altogether or may use a smaller jury than twelve or permit a verdict by less than a unanimous jury. Trials by court-martial and trials for certain criminal contempts of a Federal court or for petty offenses (very minor crimes involving light sentences) are outside the scope of the Sixth Amendment, and are conducted without a jury. In all trials, state or Federal, where a jury is used it must be impartial, and no one can be excluded from jury service merely because of his race, class, or sex.

The Sixth Amendment requirement that a person "be informed of the nature and cause of the accusation" means that an accused person must be given notice in what respects it is claimed he has broken the law, in order that he may have an opportunity to prepare his defense. Generally, the accused is entitled to have all witnesses against him present their evidence orally in court; and, subject to certain exceptions, hearsay evidence cannot be used in Federal criminal trials. Moreover, the accused is entitled to the aid of the court in having compulsory process issued— usually a subpoena—which will order into court as witnesses those persons whose testimony he desires at the trial.

Amendment VII

In suits at common law, where the value in controversy shall exceed twenty dollars, the right of trial by jury shall be preserved, and no fact tried by a jury shall be otherwise re-examined in any Court of the United States, than according to the rules of the common law.

The Seventh Amendment applies only to Federal civil trials and not to civil suits in state courts. Generally speaking, if a case is brought in a Federal court and a money judgment is sought which exceeds twenty dollars, the party bringing the suit and the defendant are entitled to have the controversy decided by the unanimous verdict of a twelve-man jury.

Amendment VIII

Excessive bail shall not be required, nor excessive fines imposed, nor cruel and unusual punishments inflicted.

Whether the bail set by a lower Federal court is excessive will depend upon the facts in each particular case. In a few instances, as when a capital offense such as murder is charged, bail may be denied altogether. Whether fines or penalties are cruel or unusual must also be determined on the facts of each particular case. Torture is one form of punishment that would be deemed cruel.

Amendment IX

The enumeration in the Constitution, of certain rights, shall not be construed to deny or disparage others retained by the people.

The Ninth Amendment emphasizes the view of the Founding Fathers that powers of government are limited by the rights of the people, and that it was not intended, by expressly guaranteeing in the Constitution certain rights of the people, to recognize that government had unlimited power to invade other rights of the people.

Amendment X

The Powers Not Delegated to the United States by the Constitution, Nor Prohibited by It to the States, Are Reserved to the States Respectively, Or to the People.

The Tenth Amendment embodies the principle of federalism in that it reserves for the states the residue of powers not granted to the Federal Government or withheld from the states.

Amendment XIII, section 1

Neither slavery nor involuntary servitude, except as a punishment for crime whereof the party shall have been duly convicted, shall exist within the United States, or any place subject to their jurisdiction.

This amendment prohibited slavery in the United States. It has been held that certain state laws were in violation of this amendment because they had the effect of jailing a debtor who did not perform his obligations. The Supreme Court has ruled that selective service laws, which authorize the draft for military duty, are not prohibited by this amendment.

Amendment XIV, section 1

All persons born or naturalized in the United States, and subject to the jurisdiction thereof, are citizens of the United States and of the State wherein they reside. No State shall make or enforce any law which shall abridge the privileges or immunities of citizens of the United States; nor shall any State deprive any person of life, liberty, or property, without due process of law; nor deny to any person within its jurisdiction the equal protection of the laws.

The Fourteenth Amendment protects Americans from certain types of state action. Thus, violations of "due process" by the state and its subdivisions, such as counties, municipalities, and cities, are prohibited. Just as under the Fifth Amendment due process has procedural and substantive aspects with respect to Federal action, so also under the Fourteenth Amendment the power of a state is limited both as to what it may do and how the state may do it. The requirement of equal protection prohibits a state from making unreasonable distinctions between different persons as to their rights and privileges. For example, the Supreme Court has held that a state cannot arbitrarily deny some of its citizens the right to vote or to serve on juries. Nevertheless, the state remains free to make reasonable classifications. Thus, the Supreme Court has held in one recent case that, under certain circumstances, a state may grant voting rights to the literate, but deny them to the illiterate.

Amendment XV

The right of citizens of the United States to vote shall not be denied or abridged by the United States or by any State on account of race, color, or previous condition of servitude.

Amendment XIX

The right of citizens of the United States to vote shall not be denied or abridged by the United States or by any State on account of sex.

The intent and purpose of these two amendments is clear. The right to vote, which is the keystone of our democratic society, may not be denied to any citizen in either a state or Federal election merely because he is born into a particular group. Even today, in some democratic countries, women do not possess the voting right. These amendments, together with the Fifth and Fourteenth Amendments, prohibit any arbitrary attempt to disfranchise any American citizen.

FREE SPEECH [2]

Our nation was settled in the first place because a few stubborn religious zealots on the British Isles found they could not express their beliefs freely in their homeland. They were people of extraordinary purpose and will. And rather than suffer in silence, they chose to make a new home on the shores of colonial America.

Of course, it was not long before these same self-exiled exponents of freedom of religious speech were busy denying the same freedom to others who disagreed with them. But at least the precedent had been struck, and from these seeds, deep roots went down on this continent.

Woven throughout the entire stuggle for American independence was that persistent theme: the right to speak one's mind. It found eloquent expression in the revolutionary writings of the time, including the Declaration of Independence, and finally came to be spelled out in the amendments attached to the United States Constitution in the form of the Bill of Rights.

But I think it is important to note the context and evolutionary pattern in which this right was asserted. At first, it was little more than the right to speak one's mind in conversation with another—without being turned in as a purveyor of seditious slander—a right, incidentally, still largely denied by most authoritarian regimes even to this day.

Then it became the right to speak freely in the church or town meeting. This met the essential need at the time, because for all practical purposes, there were no larger audiences to address. But as the towns grew into cities and the frontiers were pushed back with more and more rural settlements, it became necessary to expand the right of free speech to the publication of papers and books.

It was at this juncture—with the publication of printed matter such as Peter Zenger's crusading New York *Journal*, Tom Paine's incendiary essays, Ben Franklin's impertinent penny press, and Alexander Hamilton's fundamental Federalist Papers—that the

[2] From "Freedom of Speech," address by LeRoy Collins, former Governor of Florida and president of the National Association of Broadcasters, now director of the Community Relations Service established under the 1964 Civil Rights Act. The address was delivered to the Oregon State Association of Broadcasters, Portland, November 20, 1962. Text from *Vital Speeches of the Day*. 29:220-2. Ja. 15, '63. Reprinted by permission.

right of free speech became inexorably interwoven with the right of a free press. And the more people learned to read, the more vital this right of a free press became.

As this happened, something else began to take place—something which never has been written into any constitution or bill of rights or law of any nation, and yet, has now come to be an essential part of a free society and just as precious as the expressed provision of the right of free speech—the right to hear and see.

Together, these two rights—the right to speak and write and the right to hear and see—have made up an entirely new concept among the rights of man: the right of communications.

As our society has become more and more complex with swiftly growing numbers of events and ideas, more and more it has become dependent upon mass communications. In a democracy, free mass communication has become inextricably a part of democracy, itself. This was what Jefferson had in mind when he commented that if he had to choose between a free government and a free press, he would take the free press. He well knew that without a free press, any free government would soon perish, while with a free press, regardless of other conditions, a free government would soon emerge.

You cannot strengthen the freedom to communicate without strengthening democracy. Nor can you weaken such freedom without weakening democracy.

There is not a community served by a radio or television station in America—and that covers them all—which is not in some way caught up in the great issues of our day, issues which are crying for solution.

Just as your state has become less and less a collection of isolated towns and counties, we no longer are a nation of remote independent communities. More than ever before, we are one nation indivisible. Every county with an ailing agricultural economy is a drag on the nation. So is every urban community with unresolved traffic congestion. So is every state with a malapportioned legislature. So is every illiterate person. So is every individual American who is not informed about the great social, economic and political issues of our time and, therefore, does not pull his share of the load of responsible self-government.

No force in America is better equipped than is broadcast journalism to help shed light on community problems, point ways to their solution and help equip the people of this nation to fulfill their individual responsibilities as citizens. The people of America have a right to expect from the broadcaster a high degree of performance.

But the broadcaster cannot adequately do this simply by the goodness of his intentions. Government at all levels has the responsibility to protect the freedom of communications and to help advance it. This it can do in many ways, including the opening of its own doors to full and equal coverage by all news media. This means equal access to cover proceedings with the "tools" of broadcast journalism—the microphone and the camera. Whenever this right is denied—and these barriers exist at all levels of government—the more this important right of the people to see and hear is seriously impaired.

The too-often unjustified use of the security label and the hazy doctrine of executive privilege, the substitution of the pat "handout" for first-hand inquiry by the press—these are trends, often well-intentioned, which should be reversed. Only in the rarest of cases can the "closed-door policy" of government operation be justified.

The executive branch of our Federal system has made great use of broadcasting for communicating with the people. From the days of the fireside chats to the present live presidential news conferences, the people have developed a far better understanding of the executive than of any other branch of government. And unquestionably, radio and television have made this possible.

The courts, however, cling tenaciously to a tradition of overcloister. In fact, the Rules of Criminal Procedure forbid the broadcaster to cover a criminal trial in the Federal courts under threat of jail for contempt.

It is little wonder, when the people can see and hear their President at work, and to some degree, their Congress; when they can fly with their astronauts through space; when they can see and hear arguments dealing with grave and complex international problems directly from the United Nations, that the courts are so grossly misunderstood and often, actually feared by our citizens. For what the people cannot hear and see in a free society, the people are likely to misunderstand; and what they do not understand, they are just as likely to fear and resent.

It is argued by the American Bar Association that with broadcast coverage, the participants in court trials and other governmental proceedings would "ham it up." Under fair trial tests, however, this has not proved true. Actually, I predict that fifteen years from now, this contention that under broadcast coverage, lawyers will all try to appear as Perry Masons, and judges as John Barrymores, will seem about as ludicrous in retrospect as something that happened in a Federal courtroom in New York some years ago:

A sardonic district attorney presented to a jury a glass gadget which looked something like a small electric light bulb. With masterly scorn, he accused the defendant of claiming that by use of this "worthless" device, the human voice would some day be transmitted across the Atlantic. He said that gullible investors had been persuaded by such preposterous claims to buy stock in a company and urged prison terms for the defendant and his partners. Two of his associates were convicted, but the inventor got off with a severe lecture from the judge.

The defendant in this case was Lee de Forest; the "worthless glass bulb" was the audion tube, greatest single invention of the twentieth century; the foundation of today's multibillion-dollar electronics industry; and the greatest influence for education and enlightenment in our modern world. . . .

While the means of mass communication, along with all other aspects of our society, have changed dramatically since revolutionary days, there is nothing new or strange about the truths which underlie the very foundations of the American democracy.

However, these truths—these precepts of the brotherhood of man and the dignity of the individual—must be reinterpreted by each new generation in the light of new conditions and new demands.

The capabilities of broadcasting for serving this kind of mass communication responsibility are enormous. But to do its job, broadcasting cannot carry on its back the handicap of censorship of news—whether that censorship is implied or direct, whether by government or by private interest.

More broadcasters must be willing to do more of what other broadcasters have done—that is, accept their true roles as inseparable parts of their communities, turn their attention to the knottiest of social problems besetting the people they serve, bring the full fair light of broadcast journalism to bear upon those controversial issues, take positions which they know to be right regardless of popularity, and accept the responsibilities which go with difficult judgments.

FREE PRESS [3]

The Supreme Court struck a new balance . . . [in March [1964] between two sometimes conflicting interests—the right of Americans to speak and write and publish freely and the protection of their reputations against defamatory comment.

The Constitution, the Court held, provides special protection for comment on the public performance of public officials. Even though a statement be false and defamatory, an official may not recover libel damages unless he can prove with "convincing clarity" that it was motivated by deliberate malice.

This was the rule laid down by the court in the case of *New York Times v. Sullivan*. It was a new rule, as the opinion by Justice William J. Brennan Jr., acknowledged, one designed to meet new threats to freedom of the press and freedom of speech. Its full scope will be clear only after some time and perhaps after other cases.

[The New York *Times* libel case arose out of an advertisement published by that newspaper on March 29, 1960. The advertisement sought to raise funds for civil rights causes and was signed by friends of civil rights in the North and four Negro ministers in the South, though without the knowledge of the latter. The advertisement was critical of the handling of racial demonstrations by public officials in Montgomery, Alabama. No names were mentioned, but Montgomery's police commissioner brought a libel action against the ministers and the *Times* and won an award in the circuit court of Montgomery County. Some of the ministers' property was seized and sold at sheriff's sale; and a judgment of $500,000 was made against them and the *Times* collectively. The case was reversed in a unanimous Supreme Court ruling.—Ed.]

The *Times* case should have a forceful impact on the country's press and politicians, for it allows—really requires—all con-

[3] From "Court Broadens Freedom of the Press," by Anthony Lewis, correspondent, New York *Times* Washington bureau. New York *Times*. p 10E. Mr. 15, '64. Copyright © 1964 by The New York Times Company. Reprinted by permission.

cerned to see the possibility of libel action in an entirely new light. Until now the limits on libel suits have been a matter for state law. Different states followed different rules. Many, but not all, provided a qualified privilege for criticism of public officials, along with other privileges. Standard texts on libel devoted chapters to rundowns of state law and hardly a word to the Federal Constitution.

Now there is a unform national limitation under the free press and speech clauses of the First Amendment. Its most immediate effect is likely to come in the context in which the *Times* case arose—the context of the racial struggle in the South.

What seems to have been happening in the last few years is the development of the ordinary civil libel suit into a device for the repression of critical comment on government and its officials. The Montgomery *Advertiser,* a segregation-minded paper . . . summed it up rather frankly when it headlined a story on the various libel suits against the *Times:* "State Finds Formidable Legal Club to Swing at Out-of-State Press."

As is so often the case, excess on the part of state officials has now been met by application of the Constitution to a new area. Overreaching produces a judicial reaction.

In the past, as Justice Brennan noted in his opinion for the Court . . . , the Supreme Court has looked past such lables as "insurrection," "contempt," "breach of the peace," "obscenity" and "solicitation of legal business" to find violations of the First Amendment. Now it has looked under the cover "libel" and found a device to repress free discussion of public issues.

The decision is not likely to make this country's newspapers more savage in their appraisals of politicians than they have been in the past. Some of the political cartoons and editorial assaults of the nineteenth century make today's look tame indeed. What the Court has encouraged by this elaboration of the First Amendment is outspoken press comment on the sensitive issues of the day. The Court agreed with Herbert F. Wechsler of New York, who wrote in the brief for the *Times:*

This is not a time—there never was a time—when it would serve the values enshrined in the Constitution to force the press to curtail its attention to the tensest issues that confront the country or to forgo the dissemination of its publications in the areas where tension is extreme.

Lawyers who have studied Justice Brennan's opinion do not doubt that it provides very substantial protection for critical comment on official conduct. It is true, as Justice Hugo L. Black said in his concurring opinion, that a Southern jury might find "malice" and return a huge verdict whatever the facts. But Justice Brennan made clear that the Court will scrutinize any such verdict and put a heavy burden on the official to sustain it.

Some may be concerned at the idea that an official may not recover damages for even false statements, if they were made in good faith. The reason for including the false within the privilege was given by Justice Brennan:

A rule compelling the critic of official conduct to guarantee the truth of all his factual assertions—and to do so on pain of libel judgment virtually unlimited in amount—leads to self-censorship.

The public figure remains free, moreover, to sue for defamatory comment on his private life. The only member of the Court who reads the First Amendment so broadly as to bar libel suits even in the wholly private area is Justice Black. At least he has said so in the past. He did not reach the point . . . [in this case].

The case of *New York Times v. Sullivan* permits exaggeration, error and even foolishness in the inevitably crude efforts of mankind to arrive at political truth. Its theory is that truth should be arrived at by debate in the market place of ideas. That is the theory of the First Amendment.

FREEDOM TO TRAVEL [4]

The Supreme Court took a long step [in June 1964] toward making it clear that freedom to travel enjoys constitutional protection akin to that given freedom of speech and association. The Court's invalidation of a Federal law barring passports to members of the Communist party and of groups officially designated as Communist fronts stemmed from its conviction that no such blanket limitation on the right to travel is permissible under the Constitution.

[4] From "Subversion in Travel," editorial. New York *Times.* p 32. Je. 23, '64. Copyright © 1964 by The New York Times Company. Reprinted by permission.

The decision does not, of course, handcuff Congress in dealing with the danger of communist espionage or other specific crimes. To the extent that stopping travel will protect the United States against betrayal of its secrets or illegal acts of subversion, the remedy lies in legislation much more carefully pinpointed than that struck down by the Court. But this is quite different from prohibiting the movement outside the Western Hemisphere of all Communists, without regard for the purpose of their journey or the degree of their involvment in the party.

The United States does not add to its security or to world respect for its structure of liberties by imposing such across-the-board restrictions. The Court's decision should prove salutary in encouraging the State Department as well as Congress to ease travel curbs, instead of finding excuses to tighten them.

THE RIGHT TO PRIVACY [5]

Individual privacy was perhaps the strongest single influence that guided our forefathers in establishing the rights of free men in their new United States of America. Today, 175 years later, Americans have to decide whether their basic right of privacy shall slip from their grasp through default by inaction, whether it shall be given up willingly and wittingly or whether it shall be preserved inviolate.

Illegal wiretapping, one of the most flagrant intrusions upon liberty and personal privacy, has grown in usage to considerable proportions since its development in the early 1900's. It has been cloaked in a shroud of amorphous semi-illegality and vilified by some of the nation's most eloquent and respected spokesmen on jurisprudence and law enforcement. Recently, however, wiretapping has been pictured to the public by men of considerable stature in the executive and legislative branches as an indispensable weapon against crime.

How can this sharp division of opinion exist if, as it would appear, wiretapping clearly is an invasion of the fundamental right to privacy protected by the First (free speech), Fourth (unreasonable search) and Fifth (self-incrimination) Amendments to the Constitution?

[5] From "Electronic Eavesdropping: Trespass by Device," by John T. Lynch, lawyer and former vice president of the Council of International Investigators. *American Bar Association Journal.* 50:540-4. Je. '64. Reprinted by permission.

What is wiretapping? Generally it is an interception by technical devices providing a complete search of conversations or communications, usually without the knowledge of any of the parties using the telephone, telegraph or other wire-connected communications system. What is said by all parties is secretly recorded and preserved. The recordings can be duplicated and distributed to third parties. A wiretap is usually continuous—twenty-four hours a day. In some cases wiretaps have been in operation for years and presumably are still operating. . . .

Developments in four distinct and important areas are bringing the question of wiretapping to a showdown, one which will have a profound consequence upon the American citizen's right of privacy of communication, regardless of the outcome. They are:

1. *Status of the law.* Contradictory decisions of state and Federal courts—in addition to the absence of a clear-cut pronouncement by the Supreme Court—have left some aspects of the present wiretap law in a state of confusion. Some states admit evidence obtained by one or another means of electronic trespass even when it is obtained and presented in violation of Federal statutes and constitutional law. Law-enforcement officers having primary jurisdiction have refused to prosecute complaints against police officers who are guilty of intercepting and divulging conversations obtained through wiretapping, although such action clearly is prohibited by Federal statute and the statute has been found valid by the Supreme Court.

2. *Legislative attempts to legalize wiretapping.* In recent years bills have been introduced in Congress to permit wiretapping. Many of these have had the active support of responsible and ethical law-enforcement officials, in addition to being backed by distinguished members of Congress. While virtually all the bills would provide a valuable tool for crime prevention and apprehension, some of them could open the door to a flood of secret, unwarranted intrusions into the private lives and freedom of ordinary citizens by both ethical and unethical law-enforcement officers. . . .

3. *State of the art.* Sophisticated surveillance devices, some recently developed, provide an ominous reach into individual privacy which is available to the lawless and law-enforcing elements of society alike. In fact, wiretapping as it was known only

a few years ago may soon be outmoded by these improved devices. High induction coils provide easy, undetected access to virtually all telephone conversations. Tiny transmitters broadcast every word to receiving sets distant from the conversation or tapping location. Parabolic microphones out of sight of the conferees faithfully reproduce "private" conversations.

But even these devices pale in comparison with more sophisticated and ordinarily undetectable instruments, some currently in use and others under development, which secretly photograph and record every action and word. Lip reading, a communications device dating from antiquity, becomes a modern technique performed with the aid of ultrahigh-powered telescopes. Infrared ray telescopes and film can photograph a person in darkness. Easily hidden miniature sound transmitters broadcast to tiny, transistorized, automatically actuated receiving and recording equipment. Miniature automatic still and motion-picture cameras enable trained investigators to see in darkness and hear through walls.

These devices enable, without a personal, physical presence, an intrusion upon the air, light and sound waves of a person's property as real an invasion of privacy as a television camera and sound transmitter in the middle of an individual's living room broadcasting without his consent.

4. *An uninformed nation.* Other than *The Eavesdroppers* (Rutgers University Press, 1959), by Samuel Dash, Richard F. Schwartz and Robert E. Knowlton, there [is] scant research and literature available to the public. It is alleged in some cases that police and prosecution officials have placed the wiretap operations of their departments in a top-secret category and made the operating site off-limits to regular department personnel. This practice reduces leaks of intelligence information, helps identify officers who are accepting bribes and cooperating with hoodlums, and reduces the possibility of discovery of these illegal police wiretaps. Specific leads obtained from these wiretaps often are furnished to the department's detective bureau, which is then in a position to develop and help prosecute a case without being directly tainted by the handling of the illegal tap. And who is to condemn this practice? Hoodlums and criminals?

The curtain of official silence which necessarily masks wiretapping activities by government bodies may be understandable,

if not acceptable, to many thoughtful persons. But how does this
square with the public's right to know, to be fully informed, before being asked to give sanction to a practice which indeed is
terra incognita? If permissive wiretap legislation is to be considered, the public deserves a grat deal more information about
the extent of present wiretapping by public officials than has thus
far been provided. To do less would do grave disservice to the
principle that the American people are fit to govern themselves.

When considered historically, it may be said that the 1950's
and 1960's produced the age of trespass by scientific device. In
less than a decade technology has breached the centuries-old pro-
tective bounds against self-incrimination and the right to privacy
so carefully woven into the Bill of Rights. It has changed the
very definition of the word "trespass," which for so long meant
the intrusion of a solid object on or against another solid object.
Modern physics, which defines X-rays, gamma rays or other types
of energy as much an "object" as a solid piece of iron, gives the
very air in our homes, offices, plants, shops, cars and hotel rooms,
as well as light and sound waves passing through them, the status
formerly limited to more tangible objects such as doors, windows
and walls.

In view of this definition, then, the legal question arises: Is a
technical device intruding into the air, sound, light waves or telephone lines of a person's home or office, without either his knowledge or consent, as much a physical trespass and violation of the
right to privacy as is the opening or breaking open of his door or
window and making an unlawful physical entry?

Is Wiretapping Constitutional?

The Supreme Court has said that the signers of the Constitution had no conception of the telephone, radio and other wonders
of modern science when they insisted upon the inclusion of the
Bill of Rights to protect the people in their homes from frivolous
and frequent police abuses. These amendments were inspired by
irate citizens who finally rebelled against an all-powerful government's punishing writs of assistance. They put an end to the
general warrants used by the King's men to invade the domiciles
of American colonists in a general search for evidence of a crime
—any crime, any evidence—and to arrest, seize or question a suspect without showing reasonable cause.

The fundamental bulwark between the individual and government embodied in the prohibition of self-incriminating testimony is summarily removed by today's electronic devices. In fact, more reliable testimony is provided by them than by the actual conferees, who may forget the exact words, tenor or emphasis of what was said after a period of time. Consequently, these devices may force a person to testify against himself, without his consent, knowledge or even his presence—hardly something one could imagine being endorsed by the signers of the Constitution. . . .

[But in 1928 the Supreme Court ruled, in *Olmstead v. United States,* that wiretapping was not included within the scope of either the Fourth or Fifth Amendments, and that evidence secured by wiretapping was admissible in Federal courts even if it was illegal in the state in which it occurred. To this day that decision has not been overruled. Nevertheless, the Supreme Court has repeatedly upheld the inadmissibility of evidence obtained by wiretapping by citing a few words from one section of the Federal Communications Act of 1934. Even then, however, such evidence was inadmissible only in *Federal* courts until 1957, when the Court held that no state could legalize wiretapping. It may appear, therefore, that the right to privacy from wiretapping is still guaranteed. But this protection exists only because of a ruling based on a statutory law, not because of a constitutional right. Consequently, this protection could be avoided by a simple change in or repeal of the relevant section of the Federal Communications Act of 1934. A variety of such bills has been proposed.—Ed.]

The constitutional protection of the right to privacy against unwarranted and general searches and seizures and the right to freedom of speech, when considered together, must necessarily include the right to communicate to others in private, without having conversations subjected to eavesdropping, whatever the form. When the Bill of Rights was written, there were only two principal forms of communication, the spoken word and the written word. The right to privacy in the mails, the principal form of written communication, has long been sustained by our courts. . . . The same tests apply to the spoken word. The critical question is how a wiretap can be made specific rather than general. The answer is simple. It cannot.

The danger of relaxing protection of the right to privacy perhaps was best expressed by Justice Brandeis in his famous dissent in the *Olmstead* case when he said:

Experience should teach us to be most on our guard to protect liberty when the government's purposes are beneficent. Men born to freedom are naturally alert to repel invasions of their liberties by evil-minded rulers. The greatest dangers to liberty lurk in the insidious encroachment by men of zeal, well-meaning but without understanding.

By permitting Federal and state statutes and court rulings to chip away the foundations of our basic freedoms, we are inviting further trespass by public agencies to invade the privacy and freedom of the citizen. Modern technical trespassing devices have been inviting both the lawless and well-intentioned law-enforcement officers to make a mockery of personal liberty and privacy with impunity.

EQUALITY BEFORE THE LAW [6]

For nearly two hundred years, Americans have said that the poor man is as worthy in the eyes of the law as the rich man. In 1854, the Supreme Court of Indiana said: "It is not to be thought of, in a civilized community, for a moment, that any citizen put in jeopardy of liberty, should be debarred of counsel because he was too poor to employ such aid. No court could be respected, or respect itself, to sit and hear such a trial." More than a hundred years later we are still far short of that ideal. . . .

There have been two critical questions along the way: Does the justice promised in the Constitution apply only to the Federal courts, or does it apply also to state courts? And does the justice promised by the Constitution apply to persons accused of small crimes as much as it applies to persons accused of large crimes?

The year 1931 was a desperate one. Work was scarce. People were restless and moody. They moved to be moving, and for some the freight train was a favorite vehicle. On March 25 of that year, eight Negro teen-agers climbed aboard a freight train in Alabama. Already in the open gondola car were seven white

[6] From "Justice for the Poor; The Banner of Gideon," by Robert G. Sherrill, a correspondent of the Miami *Herald*. *Nation*. 198:367-72. Ap. 13, '64. Reprinted by permission.

boys and two white girls. There was a fight. All the white boys but one were thrown off. Before the train reached Scottsboro, Alabama, a sheriff's posse was organized and waiting. The girls accused the Negroes of raping them.

At the trial, the Negroes—all illiterate—were assigned, not a particular attorney, but the *entire* bar association of Scottsboro for their defense. They were convicted, but fortunately the case made its way to the Supreme Court where it was ruled—Justice Sutherland delivering the opinion—that "all" the members of the bar could not be given "that clear appreciation of responsibility" that a particular attorney might be given, and that assigning the entire bar association for their defense was "little more than an expansive gesture."

The case is known as *Powell v. Alabama*, and it is looked back on as a landmark case because the Supreme Court interpreted Article VI of the Bill of Rights (right to counsel) as applying to state courts as well as Federal. True, the Court pushed it no further than in capital cases, but it was a beginning. Many states already had such guarantees, either by statute or by constitutional provision, but these guarantees were sometimes ignored, as in this case. And heretofore, if the state courts wanted to execute defenseless persons, that was the state's business. *Powell v. Alabama* made it Federal business. . . .

Twice again in the 1930's the Court reaffirmed its position.

Then, in 1941 . . . the Supreme Court made an unexpected switch. Smith Betts, an unemployed farm hand with little education, was accused of burglary in Carroll County, Maryland, and tried without a jury. He was also tried without the aid of a defense lawyer, since in Carroll County indigents didn't get free legal aid unless they were charged with murder or rape. He defended himself as well as he could: calling witnesses, cross-examining, making motions and objections. He went at it with a plodding will. But he was convicted and sentenced to eight years. He claimed his constitutional privileges had been abridged by the failure to supply counsel, and he appealed to the Supreme Court.

Now for the first time the Court was squarely confronted with the question: If in capital cases, why not in felony cases? The question was answered in the negative. The court decided that

legal counsel was called for only in capital cases and that lawyers were not required for the indigent in state courts except in
capital cases.

The third act of the drama, whose first two acts were played
principally in Alabama and Maryland, remained in the Deep
South. . . .

Clarence Gideon, a wispy middle-aged nobody who earns a
living as an electrician, was convicted in Panama City, Florida, . . . of burglarizing a pool room. Like Betts, he fought his
courtroom fight without the aid of an attorney, although, like
Betts, he had asked for help. Gideon lost and, sitting in Raiford
penitentiary, he started mailing out his neatly hand-printed appeals. They were rejected regularly, until his appeal reached the
Supreme Court.

March 18, 1963, was a great day for the paupers. Handed
down that day by the United States Supreme Court were opinions that a pauper has a right to a free transcript of his trial record, for appeal purposes, even if his court-appointed attorney says
it wouldn't do any good; that paupers are entitled to free tran-
scripts of the court record even if the judge feels their appeal
would be frivolous and a waste of public money; and that a convicted person must be supplied with an attorney to help him file
his appeal.

But the fourth and most explosive decision handed down that
day carried the title *Gideon v. Wainwright*. Louie Wainwright is
director of the Florida prison system, whom Gideon considered
his improper keeper. The Supreme Court agreed. Demolishing
the old Betts decision, it ruled that no jail should hold Gideon
until he had had a trial balanced between prosecution and
defense.

[Eventually Gideon had his trial, with counsel, and as it
turned out he was acquitted. Subsequently, the courts in Florida
and many other states were besieged with writs from other prisoners. So far, in Florida, 1,118 prisoners have left the penitentiary, some to freedom and some to await new trials. Of the 321
retried so far, 12 have received longer sentences, 77 their original
sentences, and 232 reduced sentences. Of those who have been
freed, only 48 have committed new crimes.—Ed.]

THE RIGHT TO EQUAL JUSTICE [7]

I cannot help but be concerned as to whether, despite the efforts of dedicated public officials and conscientious lawyers—there is in fact equal justice before the law here in the United States. I am speaking now of a concern for whether there is true equality in the administration justice. . . .

Do members of ethnic or political minorities or people who speak our language imperfectly or who have low mentality or disturbed minds; or the largest group, those who are poor, really receive the same protection before the courts as the rest of our citizens? I say that all too often they do not.

I need hardly to say . . . that everyone in this land—whether immigrant or pauper, alleged crook or Communist—is innocent until proven guilty and is entitled to as fair a trial and as competent representation as say, leading citizens accused of price-fixing in business or of corruption in labor. It seems to me that our obligation . . . is to make the assurance of fair and equal treatment to all before the law one of our first concerns.

Judge Learned Hand, speaking at the seventy-fifth anniversary of the Legal Aid Society of New York, said if we are to keep our democracy, there must be one commandment: "Thou shalt not ration justice."

Let me discuss . . . just a few of the areas which must cause us all concern. One is the problem of the representation of indigent defendants. This is not a problem of charity, but of justice.

Mr. Justice Black points out in *Griffin v. Illinois*, "there can be no equal justice where the kind of trial a man gets depends upon the amount of money he has." This is true not only at the time of trial, but during the entire range of legal procedure until the last issue is resolved. . . .

Last year, almost 30 per cent of the defendants in the 34,008 criminal cases in Federal court could not afford counsel. In the District of Columbia, where the Federal District Court hears all felony cases, over half the defendants had to be assigned attorneys. The situation in the states is comparable. Federal and most state

[7] From "Judicial Administration," address delivered by Senator Robert F. Kennedy (Democrat, New York), then Attorney General of the United States, to the American Bar Association, San Francisco, August 6, 1962. Text from *Vital Speeches of the Day.* 28:706-8. S. 15, '62. Reprinted by permission.

jurisdictions now hold that the right to counsel at trial is an affirmative right which must be extended by the Government when the defendant cannot provide his own. . . .

The provision of counsel is indispensable to a democratic system of justice. But translating this principle into practice is difficult. As with most problems, one of the stumbling blocks is lack of money.

And as . . . [a recent study commissioned by the Department of Justice] discovered the problem does not end by merely providing an attorney. There are the added frequently expensive problems such as bail, pretrial investigations and appeal.

The problem of bail for instance is one that has received too little attention. . . . [The study mentioned above] has established conclusively that the question of whether a man will be kept in jail pending trial or be free is directly influenced by how wealthy he is.

A study of cases in the Southern District of New York indicates that over one third of those required to post bail of $500 or less could not do so. When the bail was set between $500 and $1500, over half were unable to post it. And there is reason to believe that many of those unable to provide bail presented no substantial risk of nonappearance. Their poverty deprived them of their liberty.

Further, the problem of establishing innocence during the crucial pretrial period was made that much more difficult. Bail protects the interests of society in assuring a defendant's appearance at trial and it also protects the interests of the individual in allowing him to be free to establish his innocence. But the indigent defendant who cannot offer security for his appearance is denied this opportunity. He cannot provide for his family and for his defense, and cannot take an active part to prove his innocence.

Preliminary studies in the Southern District of New York also indicate that those who cannot make bail are more often convicted and receive stiffer sentences than those who can.

The rights of the indigent after the trial is over—in the appeal stage—is equally a matter of concern. A series of court decisions in the last twenty years has greatly expanded the responsibility of society to help the indigent perfect his appeal.

He is now pledged virtually the same treatment as one who can pay, and this is as it must be.

But, again, the problem of translating this right into reality is difficult. Appellate work is time-consuming and requires the highest professional ability. It usually is an undue burden to call upon counsel, who has contributed his services at trial, to continue on appeal without compensation. Competent new counsel is sometimes difficult to obtain. . . .

We have come a long way since 1876 when a group of German immigrants banded together in New York to form the first Legal Aid Society, but we have not come far enough. Since 1937, the Department of Justice and for many years the American Bar Association have supported legislation which would appropriate funds to help indigent defendants in Federal courts. Now twenty-five years later it is still pending before the judiciary committees of both houses of Congress. The time to translate good intentions into law is long overdue. . . .

Another problem which is closely related and in some ways is even more difficult is the defense of those who do not fall in the category of indigent but who have limited resources available for their defense. Over 40 per cent of our families have incomes of less than $5,000 a year. These families cannot bear the cost of a complicated and extended trial and appeal which could easily equal their annual income.

Indeed, it can be the case that an indigent defendant, through the services of a first-rate volunteer attorney, may receive a better defense than one who pays a small fee and gets incompetent or indifferent counsel.

Legal services, particularly defense in criminal cases, are not like houses or automobiles where those with more money can buy better products without affecting the basic functioning of society. When one defendant cannot afford a complete defense justice is being rationed. . . .

The amount of money which can be expended on defense should not affect the outcome of the trial. If justice is priced in the market place, individual liberty will be curtailed and respect for law diminished.

IV. NEW RIGHTS AND UNIVERSAL RIGHTS

EDITOR'S INTRODUCTION

It is not surprising that during the period of the mid-century civil rights movement thought has been directed to the question of "new" rights. As was seen in Section I, the Negro drive for legal equality has quickly moved to wider economic and social needs and demands, and this has tended to broaden the general conception of rights. America's new concern about civil rights is, moreover, only a part of a world-wide interest in human rights, as is shown in the concluding selections in this section.

The question of whether new rights are needed, or are emerging, is examined in the first three articles by Carl J. Friedrich, a past president of the American Political Science Association, who deals with the matter in general terms; by Robert Theobald, who is concerned about establishing a right to an income in the light of the vast technological changes which he foresees in our economy; and by a professor of law, William P. Murphy, who deals with a more specific topic, that of academic freedom for the teaching profession.

In the next selection, two legal authorities report on institutions which have been developed in Western Europe for dealing with human rights on a supranational level. This is followed by an article by a United States State Department official, Richard N. Gardner, who examines the work of the United Nations with respect to human rights. America's concern for civil rights, foreshadowed in the Declaration of Independence, has always had a universal overtone. "That all men are created equal," reads the Declaration; Mr. Gardner considers whether United States foreign policy lives up to that principle in fostering universal human rights.

Last, the Universal Declaration of Human Rights promulgated by the United Nations is reproduced.

RIGHTS, LIBERTIES, FREEDOMS [1]

When President Roosevelt proclaimed the "Four Freedoms"
in 1941, he accepted a new conception of human rights far removed from the natural rights of the seventeenth and eighteenth
centuries . . . , [which] were largely concerned with protecting
the individual person against governmental power. . . .

In the course of the nineteenth century it gradually became
clear that such rights were not something absolute and un-
changeable. As the rationalist beliefs of the preceding age acquired historical perspective, rights were recognized as constitutionally created and guaranteed. Comparisons of different "bills
of rights" reinforced the conviction that such rights varied from
time to time and from place to place. Their adoption was seen
as not merely an act of recognizing them, but of formulating
and establishing them. . . . Natural rights thus gradually were
transformed into "civil liberties," the range of activities of the
citizen. This process was, of course, closely linked to the forward
march of democratization, and a marked shift in the assortment
of such rights occurred, as the right to vote and participate in
government and public policy formation became generally recognized and extended to the underprivileged and to women. . . .

In the more advanced democratic countries, those rights which
served the political function of better enabling the citizen to
participate—freedom of the press, of assembly and of association
—often summed up in the general freedom of expression, moved
into the foreground of attention, while the right of property was
subjected to restrictions and limitations arising from the widely
felt need for greater social control and for restraining the concentration of economic power. . . . Liberalism in its broadest
connotation was the belief in these civil liberties and in the
need for constitutionally protecting them. . . . [This was a] notion grounded in the conviction that freedom required social and
political organization which would overcome both natural and
man-made obstacles to the realization of individual freedom. . . .

Freedom of independence was [thus] being crowded by freedom of participation. This freedom of participation was actually

[1] From "Rights, Liberties, Freedoms—a Reappraisal," the presidential address de-
livered by Carl J. Friedrich to the American Political Science Association, New York,
September 5, 1963. Text from the *American Political Science Review*. 57:841-54. D. '63.
Reprinted by permission.

the older of the two. In the Greek cities it was this freedom rather than that of a personal sphere which had inspired such noble utterances as Pericles' Funeral Oration. The freedom of self-determination of "peoples" which the Draft Covenant of the Human Rights Convention of the UN proclaims in its Article 1 (though it is not included in the Universal Declaration) is a modern version of this ancient freedom of classical Greece: the freedom of each man to live under a government belonging to the same national group as he himself does and participating therein. . . . [See the United Nations Declaration of Human Rights, this section, below.]

The civil liberties, including the right of self-determination, have, however, in the twentieth century been rivaled not only by the older personal rights, but also by the *freedoms* suggested in the Rooseveltian proclamation and embodied in quite a few of the postwar constitutions as well as the United Nations' Universal Declaration of Human Rights. These new freedoms are rights of an economic and social character which characteristically involve collective and more especially governmental effort. Among these rights are the right to social security, to work, to rest and leisure, to education, to an adequate standard of living, to participation in cultural life, and even to an international order ensuring these rights. These rights, which have come into prominence in the twentieth century, actually appeared among other "natural" rights at an early date [e.g., the French Declaration of May 29, 1793]. . . . But the emphasis at that time and especially after the revolutionary fervor had subsided was upon the rights *against* the government and as the nineteenth century progressed toward democracy, upon the rights *within* the government.

Only in the twentieth century has the full significance of these social and economic rights become manifest. Such rights are obviously not protecting the individual against the government or other powerwielders, but call upon the public powers that be to see to it that such liberty as man possesses by himself is implemented by another set of freedoms which in contrast to those of independence and participation may be called freedoms of creation. They are rights which provide man with the freedom from fear and the freedom from want, that is to say they liberate him from restrictions and inhibitions which hinder his full development as a human being. While radically different from the older freedoms, they are nonetheless rightfully claimed for all men *qua* men. When Anatole France wrote his bitter quip about every Frenchman's freedom to sleep in the open under the bridges over the Seine, he was asking for such implementation. . . .

Recognizing these rights as true rights must not prevent their being seen as different from the older rights. In order to appreciate fully this difference between the three sets of rights, as evolved in the history of the last three hundred years, it is necessary first of all to determine what they have in common. If one takes these three rights, the right to one's religious conviction, the right to vote and the right to work—three rights which illustrate the freedom of independence, the freedom of participation and the freedom of creation, invention and innovation—one finds that like the corresponding freedoms these rights are all related to enabling a human being to become a rounded self, a fully developed person. Not to be allowed to believe what one does believe, not to express a preference for the ruler by whom one is in fact ruled, not to be active in the sphere in which one could produce and create anew—every one of these deprivations is readily recognized as dehumanizing, as crippling the man so afflicted and preventing him from being a person in the full sense.

That it may be difficult to implement such a proclaimed right does not invalidate it, any more than the failure to claim a right makes it disappear. The rights which the Negroes now claim in the United States have been theirs for a long time and the claims are based upon this very fact. Rights have an objective existence; they flow existentially from the very nature of man, as do the freedoms which correspond to them. For these freedoms are the manifestation of the power of human beings, of their capacity to put them to some account. There no doubt exists a wide range of difference between individual human beings in this capacity, but all men are capable of religious conviction, of voting, of working—to stay with our illustrations. The fact that each of the rights may be expressed as a capacity, as a power of man to achieve self-realization, is the hard core of all rights. Hence we may say that the most comprehensive right is this right to self-realization which has also been simply called the right to freedom.

Looked at in this perspective of the individual, rights appear to be either self-preserving, self-asserting or self-developing. Looked at in the perspective of the political order of the community, such rights are either rights apart from this political order of the community, rights within or toward the political order, or rights depending upon the political order. . . .

These classes of rights are not sharply delimited and cannot be pricisely separated from each other. . . . [For example] a right may be legally recognized and deeply felt by the person deprived of it; yet the deprivation may be caused by a non-governmental power-holder and -wielder. In that case, what appears at first to be a right apart from the political order may turn out to be a right depending upon the political order. This is typically the situation of underprivileged minorities, such as the Negroes in the United States. . . . Often the distinction between the different rights is relative to the status of the particular person in the social order. Thus, the inherent right to an education is for a wealthy person a right apart from the political order, while for the poor one it is a right depending upon the political order. . . . Such active role of the government is also recognized as needed in the economic sphere. . . .

By stressing the role of the government in the maintenance of freedom, . . . [European neoliberalism and American progressivism contribute their] share to an understanding of the fact that all rights are political in the sense of depending upon the political order for their maintenance and enforcement. They are political, however, in the further sense of depending upon the values and beliefs of the political community which the order serves. Many of the newer rights are evidently the corollary of fairly recent developments; thus the right to work could only be recognized when industrialization created large-scale unemployment. Still, it would be a mistake to make this the ground for asserting that this right only came into being at that point. Rather, the assertion of the right is rooted in the belief that it is part of man's nature to work and that therefore any situation which deprives him of fulfilling this natural propensity ought to be corrected. This reflection reinforces the important insight already mentioned that rights are characteristically normative in the sense that they reflect a tension between what is and what ought to be. From this vantage point, it can be seen that a right is related to an aspect of human nature which is being inhibited or thwarted. . . .

All creative freedom rests upon the observed fact that human beings do not only choose between existing alternatives, do not only select and prefer what is offered and available to them. When none of the available alternatives are acceptable, a new one may be discovered or invented which solves the problem, be it political or other. There is a very great difference between choosing one of several known alternatives and discovering or inventing a new one. The latter act, symbolized by procreation, is unpredictable and shrouded in mystery, yet it is undeniably an exercise of human freedom in the highest sense. Indeed, in some of its most extraordinary manifestations it is part of man's joy at play. The playful exploration of the unknown is the finest act of human freedom. It presupposes freedom from want and freedom from fear.

It may be objected here that want and fear have been powerful stimulants of great works of art and literature and there is no gainsaying this observation. But every one of these instances is exceptional in personal terms, while for most human beings neither fear nor want beyond a low limit are stimulating; they are paralyzing. If, therefore, these two freedoms are accepted, not only as the prevalent beliefs, but also as genuinely related to the over-all freedom of self-realization, it becomes a major problem of any contemporary political order how to combine them with the rights which had been recognized earlier. . . . The older constitutional systems are particularly in need of revision and radical innovation. Advance is needed, and it is more likely to be achieved at polls or constitutional conventions than in courts; it is part of the *political* process to achieve them.

The American Bill of Rights, so called, is no longer adequate. Not only has there been a certain attenuation of older rights which need to be reaffirmed and strengthened, but some of the new rights urgently require constitutional sanction. Thus the right to an adequate education, guaranteed in a number of the newer constitutions as well as the United Nations' Declaration, ought to be positively affirmed in the United States Constitution. It would provide the courts with the necessary ground for coping with certain grave abuses, such as the withholding of education from broad classes of citizens, because of local dissatisfaction with the standards (desegregation) demanded under the Constitution. The right to be educated is possibly an even more important right than the right to be admitted to a particular school. Similarly, the right to work, while promoted by much Federal legislation, may be denied by state and local authorities, when only their jurisdiction is involved. . . . Anyone comparing the traditional bill of rights derived from the eighteenth and nineteenth centuries with the modern bill of rights, making full allowance for social rights, will appreciate the need for radical revision.

But even when every effort is being made to reshape the constitutionally guaranteed rights in accordance with a wider and more adequate conception of human freedom, the problem remains of how to combine the several rights, liberties and freedoms into a balanced and harmonious whole. This problem cannot be solved in arranging these rights, liberties and freedoms into a rank list of simple priorities. The problem is not one-dimensional and static, but multidimensional and dynamic. It can only be solved in approximation and through adequate procedures for its resolution in response to specific situations and particular circumstances. . . . For example, regulatory provisions protecting the individual's freedom of expression (speech) over the air may interfere with the private property rights of the owner of the broadcasting facilities.

Not only property rights, but other rights, may be in conflict. Freedom of the press clashes with the right of privacy, as well as the right to a fair trial and other rights; many other examples could be adduced, especially as between the older rights which are self-preserving and the newer rights which are self-developing. The reasons are not far to seek; for the former favor the well-to-do *beati possidentes* [those blessed with wealth], while the latter favor the poor. It is in the very nature of such rights that they cannot be ranked in a fixed order, because the more or less in each case must be taken into account. A small infringement of a right A entailing a great loss in a right C, for example, may call for one decision, while the reverse may call for the opposite. "Situation sense" on the part of judges, legislators and administrators will be required at all times; carefully elaborated procedures which make the cautious weighing of alternatives possible are the only way of securing maximum realization of all the different rights a civilized community may recognize as worthy of protection. . . .

What, then, may we hope? The fact that rights are ever more universally recognized, even by those who seem least inclined to make them a reality, is the great distinguishing characteristic of our time. It justifies us in the hope that human rights will become more broadly descriptive of the actual behavior of men and governments; that even the right to an effective international and supranational order will gradually come within man's grasp and that thereby the ultimate condition of human freedom, the freedom from fear, will come to prevail. Such hopes would, however, . . . [be only utopian dreams], unless they are accompanied by the humble recognition of man's greater duties as his rights increase.

THE RIGHT TO AN INCOME [2]

The Western world professes impeccable ideals in the field of human rights, but nobody would attempt to deny that we have failed to live up to them. . . . The continued presence in America of 60 million people whose daily experience is a level of nutrition, education, housing and opportunity for self-fulfillment far below that considered normal by themselves and others, coupled with similar evidence from other Western countries, argues the extent of our failure.

I intend to state unequivocally . . . that only a full commitment to, and implementation of, our ideals will enable Western societies to survive in today's world of emerging abundant production through technological complexity. . . . I will not try to set out . . . the degree to which the organization of human activities may be taken over by automated machinery and computers (the cybernated system). . . . [But the revolution in cybernetics does suggest that the traditional economic patterns will no longer support the achievement of human rights to which we are dedicated.]

The Western world has so far refused to confront the problem of the distribution of resources directly. It continues to act on the belief that the only proper way for the vast majority of the pop-

[2] From "Food, Jobs and Human Rights," address by Robert Theobald, economist and free-lance consultant, to the American Association for the United Nations, DePaul University, Chicago, September 21, 1963. *Vital Speeches of the Day.* 30:61-4. N. 1, '63. Reprinted by permission.

ulation to command resources is through holding a conventional job. This means that while the well-educated and highly-skilled American worker receives a salary which enables him to live in conditions of ease and often luxury, the ill-educated and poorly-trained worker receives a wage which is only adequate to provide minimum living standards—and even this income is only available if the worker can find a job. When he cannot, and this is increasingly the case for those with the least education, the worker falls into . . . [the] culture of poverty and the affluent society promptly banishes him to the slums of the city or the poverty-stricken depressed areas of the countryside.

Recognizing this connection between jobs and income, a hesitant step toward the development of full human rights was taken at the end of the Second World War when all Western countries recognized that so long as control over resources was dependent on holding a job, society had an obligation to provide jobs for everybody. The American commitment to the goal of full employment was expressed in the Employment Act of 1946 but it has recently proved a dead letter. No effective action has been taken to eliminate the growth in unemployment rates since the mid-1950's. For the first time in a period of prosperity, the American economy is continuously failing to absorb the new entrant to the labor force. The unemployment rate for teen-agers has recently reached an historical high and is three times the national average. The unemployment rate for Negro teen-agers is about six times the national average and even rises well above 50 per cent in certain racially segregated districts in some parts of the country.

I believe that our goal must be to restore full employment in the immediate future, because the present demand of the civil rights movement for good education, housing and recreation facilities as well as adequate incomes cannot be satisfied until full employment is restored. In present conditions of continuing unemployment the lag in Negro employment can only be made up by a deliberate worsening of the employment position of other groups. This must inevitably lead to severe racial strife.

It is possible to attain full employment in the short run but not without a drastic change in economic policies. Full employment requires that government measures be taken which will provide the funds, on a national basis, to activate latent demand for private consumption by the poor and which will also accelerate the development of social service areas of the economy. The achievement of full employment in present conditions therefore requires a profound alteration in our concepts about who should have the rights to use resources and this change must occur in the immediate future.

A decision to meet America's urgent needs for private consumption and public services would use all the available manpower resources and would provide a solution to many pressing problems. This period of full employment could be lengthened by taking a commitment to provide the developing countries with all the aid they could effectively absorb. Even this bold step, however, would fail to balance supply and demand for more than a few years. It is already certain that a large proportion of the children born in the fifties and sixties will never hold jobs involving the kind of work with which we are familiar today.

In the short run full employment must be achieved for this is the only context in which present problems can be solved. . . . [But] it must be recognized now that full employment cannot be maintained in the long run and that the values of economic scarcity must disappear at the same time as the institutions which arose to meet the needs of a productive system based on scarcity. The moral and social sanctions pertaining to income rights can no longer be based on job-holding.

I can see no possible alternative in this situation but to provide every individual with an absolute constitutional right to an income adequate to allow him to live with dignity. No governmental agency, judicial body or other organization whatsoever should have the power to suspend or limit any payments assured by these guarantees.

Such an absolute constitutional right to an income will recognize that in an economy where many jobs already represent makework in any social sense and where the requirements for workers will decrease in coming years, it is ludicrous to base the right to an income on an ability to find a job.

Those of you who have read [Edward] Bellamy's *Looking Backward* will appreciate the effect I anticipate following the abolition of the necessity to strive for a job. I agree with many of his arguments: in particular that it is the structure of our system which forces much of the crime and antisocial behavior. Nevertheless, a proposal that everybody should be given an income whether he works or not needs deep evaluation, for it would revolutionize our economy and society. But I know of no alternative which is adequate to deal with the fact that there will not be enough jobs to go round in coming years. . . .

A right to an income alone would be insufficient to guarantee human rights: society must also take an unlimited commitment to produce the conditions in which every individual can develop his full intellectual potential. The acceptance of this principle would make me highly optimistic for the long run. I believe that we have so far developed only a tiny proportion of the potential of most human beings. I believe that acceptance of an absolute right to an income and complete education would allow a flowering of the spirit and mind whose dimensions cannot even be guessed today.

Absolute rights to enough resources to enable an individual to live with dignity and to the full development of the individual's capacities would allow him to achieve his own patterns of meaningful activity. However, recognition of the validity of new patterns of meaningful activity would require an automation-age interpretation of the values of work and leisure. The nineteenth century concept of a man's life as a mere division between toil and respite from toil should be allowed to disappear along with the production-oriented factory organization which gave rise to such a curiously twisted version of the relationship between an individual and his society.

In the future, work will no longer be essentially a labor-payment to society but rather the full use of an individual's potential for the material benefit of his fellows and his own self-fulfillment. In the same way, leisure will no longer be simply time not spent in toiling but rather the full use of an individual's potential for the psychical benefit of his fellows and his own recreation. . . .

I want to . . . [mention also] three new human rights which seem highly important to me. . . .

The first of these human rights is that every individual should have the right to receive information undistorted by desires to mislead for purposes of public or private gain. This is, in today's world, a very novel proposal for it means that society must develop effective sanctions against individuals and groups who distort information deliberately. That such a proposal seems novel is perhaps a good measure of the degree of malfunction in our society. The framers of the American Constitution intended that the right of free speech and a free press would be a method of achieving a consensus, not a justification of deliberate distortion, with consequent fragmentation of the society.

What types of distortion am I condemning? I condemn the advertisers who play on the weakness of the individual in order to increase their sales. I condemn the propagandists of any country who unhesitatingly distort the favorable and bury the unfavorable. I condemn the academics who distort the truth as they see it in order to gain reputations or power. I condemn the chemical firms which tried to drown Rachel Carson's book *Silent Spring* in a sea of irrelevancies because they feared for their sales. I condemn the funeral directors who answered Jessica Mitford's book *The American Way of Death* in which she pleaded for dignity and restraint in funerals with a statement that Miss Mitford was trying to alter the American funeral service to conform with that practiced in communistic countries such as the Soviet Union. . . .

I believe that the existence of lively controversy which allows the discovery of the truth in constantly changing circumstances is one of the prime necessities of today. I believe that only a lively democracy can lead to the adoption of appropriate policies. I believe that concentration of power in the hands of a few is not only against our past ideals but fails to meet present necessities. . . .

The second new human right is for the individual to be provided with guarantees about the quality of all the goods he purchases. While this appears a radical step, it actually reflects present operating policies of socially responsible firms quite accurately. In earlier centuries, the purchaser was able to determine the quality, condition and quantity of the goods he was purchasing and was also able to express his attitude by haggling over price. This position persisted throughout the industrial revolution: the seller offered a product and it was the responsibility of the purchaser to determine whether it was satisfactory. This is the famous legal doctrine of *caveat emptor*: or let the buyer beware.

Today, however, the situation is entirely changed. The consumer cannot reasonably be expected to examine a television set or any other complex product to determine if it is well made: the makers of many types of goods have recognized this fact and have steadily lengthened their periods of guarantee. Today, we need to go the next step and acknowledge that the total responsibility for determining whether a product is satisfactory lies with the seller and not with the buyer, for only the seller can afford to do this. No purchaser in today's word can possibly collect all the information he needs on all the products he wants to purchase.

Each seller should therefore become responsible for the claims made on behalf of his product and should be forced to refund some multiple of the purchase price if the product did not meet his claims. In some cases, when injury to the purchaser resulted, the seller should be liable for damages. The manufacturer will therefore have a direct financial interest in living up to the claims made for his product for if he fails to do so he will lose money.

This human right would not only minimize the time wasted by the individual in unnecessary repairs, it would also meet desirable social criteria. Time is the shortest commodity in today's world for the 10 per cent of the population whose skills are most urgently required: the social system is therefore functioning badly when it requires that the time of this group should be wasted in mending defective products and by having inoperative equipment at any time when it is required. The time and money the manufacturer saves by selling unsatisfactory products is wasted many times over by the troubles of the purchaser. We need a productive system which will produce goods which will render the services for which they were designed with the minimum possible number of break-downs. . . .

The third human right I want to mention is the right to buy from any seller. The necessity for this right stems from developments which have taken place as we have moved from a socio-economic system in which economic and social decisions were inextricably intertwined to today's situation where goods and services are impersonally distributed.

Originally the buyer and seller were in close human contact and they naturally wished to choose to whom they would sell and from whom they would buy. Today, business desires to move goods and services at a profit without entangling social problems. As a result it is not only desirable but also necessary for society to state that in return for the privilege granted the businessman of being permitted to sell goods and services, he has the obligation to serve all comers. Those who do not want to accept the obligation to sell to all comers should not be granted the right to sell at all. . . .

Cybernation provides the potential for unlimited freedom but we can only grasp this potential for freedom in a totally new form of society. Failure to use this new potential for freedom will destroy our existing freedoms through the development of technological dictatorships or lead to immensely destructive world-wide warfare.

It is necessary to create a new type of society in which an individual will be given a chance to develop his personality completely. We need a new type of society based on respect for what the individual is: not on the color of his skin or his existing position in society. We need a new type of society which condemns selfishness and lying under whatever names . . . [they] may be disguised.

Above all, we need a new form of society which recognizes the necessity for diversity. We need to accept and find ways to support the person who likes a job in a factory, the person who wishes to produce better goods and services, the person who wishes to teach, the person who wishes to work on an abstruse scientific problem whose solution appears useless, the person who wishes to beautify his garden or a corner plot, the person who wishes to back unpopular causes. We need to understand that the values of these people may be entirely different, that some may wish to work sixty hours a week and some twenty, some may be content with a relatively small income, others will need large sums.

We need in fact to reconsider all our policies in the light of the fundamental goal of Western societies which is to ensure that each individual has the maximum freedom of action in his choice of action which is compatible with the needs of the society. We have to see how this goal can be achieved in a complex technological society which will allow effectively unlimited production.

AN EMERGING CONSTITUTIONAL RIGHT [3]

[While the case for academic freedom is a powerful one, judges have not begun to demonstrate any serious appreciation of what it is all about. Among factors responsible for this state of affairs is the fact that the academic world has not sufficiently stressed the need and importance of academic freedom. Second, the freedom is almost invariably invoked for suspect persons whose conduct is considered unattractive or undesirable in some way by the community at large.] A third reason why the courts have not accorded more respect to the claims of academic freedom is, I believe, the failure of the academic community to vigorously and collectively press claims before the courts. . . .

[But] a series of recent decisions by the United States Supreme Court has opened up the possibility of a substantial degree of judicial protection of academic freedom as a right recognized and guaranteed by the United States Constitution. To the extent that academic freedom may be a matter of constitutional right, it should serve effectively to remove . . . two obstacles to judicial protection . . . , namely, the difficulty in framing a legal cause of action and the reluctance of courts to intervene in the internal affairs of an educational institution. . . .

It must be borne in mind, however, that any protection of academic freedom which may flow from the provisions of the Constitution would be confined to public institutions. Constitutional limitations run against action by government, not against private individuals or associations. The "state action" concept would obviously include action by the governing boards of state colleges and universities and would just as clearly seem to exclude action by privately endowed institutions of learning. Of course, if the act of the private institution was required by the state then the Constitution would be applicable. As it happens, however, it is by action of the governing boards in the state colleges and universities that academic freedom is most frequently violated. . . .

[Most definitions, although varied in emphasis] define academic freedom in terms of study, research, opinion, discussion, expression, publication, speech, teaching, writing, and communication. To one

[3] From "Academic Freedom—An Emerging Constitutional Right," by William P. Murphy, professor of law, University of Missouri. *Law and Contemporary Problems.* 28:448-86. Summer '63. Reprinted from a symposium, *Academic Freedom,* by permission from Law and Contemporary Problems, published by the Duke University School of Law, Durham, N.C. Copyright © 1963, by Duke University.

familiar with constitutional law but who had never heard of academic freedom, these terms would instantly fall within a familiar framework, the great and indispensable freedom which the First Amendment protects against abridgment by Congress, and which is considered so fundamental to a system of liberty and justice that it is included in the due process clause of the Fourteenth Amendment and thus made a limitation on the powers of the states. Indeed, academic freedom as so defined seems to fall so naturally and readily and logically within the ambit of constitutionally protected speech and communication that it would be surprising, in fact, if academic freedom had not been brought within the scope of the First and Fourteenth Amendments. It is clear from the jurisprudence of the past twenty-five years that the Supreme Court is committed, and one may say with some confidence irrevocably committed, to a liberal application of these amendments. . . . Educational freedom is perhaps the most important aspect of intellectual freedom, and among the educational freedoms none are more important than academic freedom, the freedom of the teacher. It would be passing strange if the Supreme Court had not come eventually to recognize within its broad view of intellectual freedom one of the vital components.

Let us look, therefore, at the opinions through which the Court has recognized academic freedom as a constitutional right. This can be done conveniently by briefly noting four of the Court's decisions, all rendered during the 1950's.

In *Adler v. Board of Education*, the Court upheld the constitutionality of a section of the New York Civil Service Law, implemented by the so-called "Feinberg Law." These sections together provided for the disqualification and removal from the public school system of teachers and other employees who advocated the overthrow of the government by unlawful means or who belonged to organizations which had such a purpose. The gist of Justice [Sherman] Minton's majority opinion stated that.

A teacher works in a sensitive area in a schoolroom. There he shapes the attitude of young minds toward the society in which they live. In this, the state has a vital concern. It must preserve the integrity of the schools. That the school authorities have the right and the duty to screen the officials, teachers, and employees as to their fitness to maintain the integrity of the schools as a part of ordered society, cannot be doubted.

Justice [William O.] Douglas wrote a dissenting opinion, concurred in by Justice [Hugo L.] Black. It is important in this study because it is the first opinion by a Supreme Court Justice to expressly recognize academic freedom as a constitutional right. Justice Douglas said in part:

The Constitution guarantees freedom of thought and expression to everyone in our society. All are entitled to it; and none needs it more than the teacher.

The public school is in most respects the cradle of our democracy. . . . The impact of this kind of censorship in the public school system illustrates the high purpose of the First Amendment in freeing speech and thought from censorship. . . .

The very threat of such a procedure is certain to raise havoc with academic freedom. . . . Fearing condemnation, [the teacher] will tend to shrink from any association that stirs controversy. In that manner freedom of expression will be stifled. . . .

There can be no real academic freedom in that environment. Where suspicion fills the air and holds scholars in line for fear of their jobs, there can be no exercise of the free intellect. . . .

This system of spying and surveillance with its accompanying reports and trials cannot go hand in hand with academic freedom. It produces standardized thought, not the pursuit of truth. Yet it was the pursuit of truth which the First Amendment was designed to protect. . . . We need be bold and adventuresome in our thinking to survive. . . . The framers knew the danger of dogmatism; they also knew the strength that comes when the mind is free, when ideas may be pursued wherever they lead. We forget these teachings of the First Amendment when we sustain this law.

Justice [Felix] Frankfurter, dissenting for jurisdictional reasons, nevertheless paid respect to "the teacher's freedom of thought, inquiry, and expression," and to "the freedom of thought and activity, and especially . . . the feeling of such freedom, which are, as I suppose no one would deny, part of the necessary professional equipment of teachers in a free society."

The same year in which it upheld the New York law the Court, in *Wieman v. Updegraff,* invalidated an Oklahoma statute requiring all state officers and employees to take loyalty oaths that they were not, and had not been for the preceding five years, members of organizations listed by the United States Attorney General as Communist front or subversive. The requirement was struck down because of its indiscriminate classification of innocent with knowing membership in such organizations. The action had been commenced because certain members of the faculty and staff at Oklahoma Agricultural and Mechanical College had refused to take the oath. This circumstance prompted Justice Frankfurter to write a separate concurring opinion in which Justice Douglas joined. It is worth quoting at some length:

. . . to require such an oath, on pain of a teacher's loss of his position in case of refusal to take the oath, penalizes a teacher for exercising a right of association peculiarly characteristic of our people. . . . Such joining is an exercise of the rights of free speech and free inquiry. By limiting the power of the states to interfere with freedom of speech and freedom of inquiry and freedom of association, the Fourteenth Amendment protects all persons, no matter what their calling. But, in view of the nature of the teacher's relation to the effective exercise of the rights which are safeguarded by the Bill of Rights and by the Fourteenth Amendment, inhibition of freedom of thought, and of action upon thought, in the case of teachers brings the safeguards of those amendments vividly into operation. Such unwarranted inhibition upon the free spirit of teachers affects not only those who, like the appellants, are immediately before the Court. It has an unmistakable tendency to chill that free play of the spirit which all teachers ought especially to cultivate and practice; it makes for caution and timidity in their associations by potential teachers. . . .

That our democracy ultimately rests on public opinion is a platitude of speech but not a commonplace in action. Public opinion is the ultimate reliance of our society only if it be disciplined and responsible. It can be disciplined and responsible only if habits of open-mindedness and of critical inquiry are acquired in the formative years of our citizens. The process of education has naturally enough been the basis of hope for the perdurance of our democracy on the part of all our great leaders, from Thomas Jefferson onwards.

To regard teachers—in our entire educational system, from the primary grades to the university—as the priests of our democracy is therefore not to indulge in hyperbole. It is the special task of teachers to foster those habits of open-mindedness and critical inquiry which alone make for responsible citizens, who, in turn, make possible an enlightened and effective public opinion. Teachers must fulfill their function by precept and practice, by the very atmosphere which they generate; they must be exemplars of open-mindedness and free inquiry. They cannot carry out their noble task if the conditions for the practice of a responsible and critical mind are denied to them. They must have the freedom of responsible inquiry, by thought and action, into the meaning of social and economic ideas, into the checkered history of social and economic dogma. They must be free to sift evanescent doctrine, qualified by time and circumstance, from that restless, enduring process of extending the bounds of understanding and wisdom, to assure which the freedoms of thought, of speech, of inquiry, of worship are guaranteed by the Constitution of the United States against infraction by national or state government.

The functions of educational institutions in our national life and the conditions under which alone they can adequately perform them are at the basis of these limitations upon state and national power.

In 1957, in the case of *Sweezy v. New Hampshire,* the recognition of academic freedom as a constitutional right moved from dissenting and concurring opinions into acceptance by a majority of six members of the Supreme Court. In this case the Court reversed a conviction of contempt entered against a professor who had refused to answer questions asked by state authority concerning his connection with the Progressive party and the content of a lecture delivered at the state university. There was no majority opinion, although six Justices concurred in the result. The opinion of Chief Justice [Earl] Warren, in which Justices Black, Douglas, and [William J.] Brennan concurred, stated:

The state supreme court thus conceded without extended discussion that petitioner's right to lecture and his right to associate with others were constitutionally protected freedoms which had been abridged through this investigation. . . . These are rights which are safeguarded by the Bill of Rights and the Fourteenth Amendment. We believe that there unquestionably was an invasion of petitioner's liberties in the areas of academic freedom and political expression—areas in which government should be extremely reticent to tread. . . .

Justice Frankfurter wrote a separate concurring opinion in which Justice [John Marshall] Harlan joined. This opinion stated that,

When weighed against the grave harm resulting from governmental intrusion into the intellectual life of a university, such justification for compelling a witness to discuss the contents of his lecture appears grossly inadequate. . . . In these matters of the spirit inroads on legitimacy must be resisted at the incipiency. This kind of evil grows by what it is allowed to feed on.

The last case to be noted . . . is *Barenblatt v. United States.* Here the Court, by a five-to-four decision, upheld the contempt conviction of a professor who had refused to answer questions concerning his membership in the Communist party propounded by a subcommittee of the House Committee on Un-American

Activities. The majority opinion, written by Justice Harlan, distinguished the case from *Sweezy* in that the Communist party and the Progressive party were "very different thing[s]" and that the interrogation as to the content of a lecture was a factor absent from the *Barenblatt* case. What interests us here, however, is the fact that at the very beginning of his opinion, Justice Harlan stated that,

> Of course, broadly viewed, inquiries cannot be made into the teaching that is pursued in any of our educational institutions. When academic teaching-freedom and its corollary learning-freedom, so essential to the well-being of the nation, are claimed, this Court will always be on the alert against intrusion by Congress into this constitutionally protected domain.

The leading dissenting opinion, written by Justice Black and joined by Chief Justice Warren and Justice Douglas, was based on broad First Amendment grounds and did not specifically discuss the existence of those freedoms in an academic context. Justice Brennan dissented separately on another ground. Since these four dissenting Justices are the same four for whom Chief Justice Warren spoke in the *Sweezy* case, it may be assumed with confidence that they agree with the statement of Justice Harlan quoted above. The *Barenblatt* case, therefore, demonstrates that, as of 1959, all nine Justices of the Supreme Court had expressly recognized academic freedom as being within the area of constitutional protection. . . .

Academic freedom has been considered in this article in its historic sense, as a freedom of the teacher. The struggle for academic freedom has demonstrated that academic tenure and due process are the means essential to achieving that great end. In this struggle constitutional law can become an important support in public institutions, through the requirement of a hearing prior to a teacher's discharge and by prohibiting certain reasons for discharge. Tenure thus becomes to some extent constitutionally protected. As between the two forms of assistance constitutional law can give to academic freedom, the procedural is probably more important than the substantive. For surely the summary discharge is the most drastic and effective technique in stifling academic freedom. It is safe to say that many discharges would never have occurred if a hearing had been required and the reasons brought into the open.

Constitutional protection of due process in teacher termination cases needs no more than the willingness of courts to require in the academic community what they have required in a host of other contexts—the elemental decency and justice of a right to notice and hearing before action is taken. There is no reason why the most venerable of our constitutional rights should be wanting in public institutions of learning. With or without a hearing, however, experience demonstrates that teachers continue to be discharged for their beliefs, associations, teaching, speaking and writing. Constitutional law can proscribe such reasons, and confine the bases of discharge to those which are relevant to the teacher's fitness and competence.

But constitutional law can never be more than an occasional valuable ally in the struggle for academic freedom. For various practical and legal reasons, judicial intervention cannot reasonably be hoped for except in the extreme case of termination of employment. And yet there are many techniques of harassment short of termination which may be used to penalize a teacher—refusal to promote or to increase salary are two of the most common. To combat and redress all the myriad ways in which academic freedom may be undermined and thwarted will always require vigilant and determined self-help activity within the academic community itself. For this the law will never be a substitute.

In addition, many cases in which constitutional law might help will never be brought for various personal reasons. Litigation is an expensive and lengthy ordeal which the aggrieved professor may be unwilling to undergo. Or he may be so thoroughly disgusted with the institution that he no longer has any desire to stay and "fight it out" and simply wants to go elsewhere. Finally, even in a termination case the constitutional issue would need to be relatively clear and uncomplicated. Certainly not all discharges are for constitutionally prohibited reasons. A reading of the investigation reports of the fourteen institutions now on the censured list of the AAUP [American Association of University Professors] illustrates the point. Some of the cases were in the area of refusal to answer questions relating to former Communist membership. Some are a tangled skein of personality differences, conflicts over educational policy, and the like. In others a semblance of a hearing was held. In the judgment of the AAUP, academic freedom, tenure, or due process was violated in each case, but many are not, for one reason or another, constitutional law cases. . . .

The Courts, in the long run, neither can nor should be ignored by the academic community. Although their assistance is not likely to be forthcoming in any but extreme cases, an enlightened judicial attitude would inevitably have a wholesome effect, in the academic world and in society generally in enhancing the acceptance of and respect for academic freedom.

As yet, the Supreme Court's decisions are harbingers of what is to come, a promise of protection yet to be redeemed. What is needed now is a decision from the Court squarely invalidating the termination of a teacher's employment made without a hearing or because of a violation of academic freedom. Until there is such a decision, it is probably more accurate to refer to academic freedom as an emerging constitutional right. A case involving a teacher whose employment was terminated for upholding the Court's own decision in *Brown* [*v. Topeka Board of Education*] would be a fitting vehicle to put the expressly recognized freedom on a sound footing. But whether in the racial area or not, such a decision seems to be, in the fullness of time, inevitable.

HUMAN RIGHTS IN WESTERN EUROPE [4]

American political theory has traditionally recognized universal or fundamental rights and indeed "in no other legal system has the law . . . been moulded with greater effect by higher law principles based on a specific interpretation of natural justice than American law." The Declaration of Independence proclaims, "We hold these truths to be self-evident, that all men are created equal, that they are endowed by their Creator with certain unalienable Rights, that among these are Life, Liberty and the pursuit of Happiness." And the due process guarantee of the Constitution is said to protect "personal immunities . . . 'so rooted in the traditions and conscience of our people as to be ranked as fundamental' . . . or . . . 'implicit in the concept of ordered lib-

[4] From "New Horizons for Human Rights: The European Convention, Court, and Commission of Human Rights," by Jack Greenberg, Director-Counsel, NAACP Legal Defense and Educational Fund, Inc., and Anthony R. Shalit, Jervey Fellow in Comparative Law, Columbia University. *Columbia Law Review*. 63:1384-1412. D. '63. Reprinted by permission.

erty.' " Reverence for these rights is not peculiar to the United States but is an outgrowth of a philosophical and religious heritage common to the Western democracies and shared by the [British] Commonwealth and other nations. However, in spite of the rapid interchange of ideas, values, and standards in the modern world, our constitutional jurisprudence has taken little explicit notice of the development and articulation of these rights in other countries.

In the Convention for the Protection of Human Rights and Fundamental Freedoms [which bcame effective May 18, 1954] the nations of Western Europe—including both common-law and civil-law countries—have not only reached agreement on the fundamental freedoms but have acquiesced in the creation of an internationally enforceable writ that may run against themselves, in many cases at the instance of individual petitioners. They have established a supranational authority to guarantee fundamental rights taking precedence over national law. These nations take quite seriously these rights, which are by and large also secured in our law, and their experience ought not to be ignored. However, we have as yet taken no account of this potential for infusing our jurisprudence with a new, perhaps invigorating, strain of authority. Indeed few American lawyers are even aware of these recent striking achievements of European law in the field of human rights. . . .

In 1948 the General Assembly of the United Nations adopted the Universal Declaration of Human Rights [see last selection, this section, below]. The spirit and much of the text of this Declaration was expressly reaffirmed by the European Convention for the Protection of Human Rights and Fundamental Freedoms. Although the Declaration has the moral authority of a unanimously adopted proclamation of the Assembly, no nation is required to obey it and no machinery exists for its enforcement. On the other hand, the Convention sets up an enforceable, international legal system that may be invoked at the petition of aggrieved individuals. Indeed, the Convention is specifically intended to take "first steps for the collective enforcement of certain of the Rights stated in the Universal Declaration."

The Council of Europe whose members signed the Convention arose out of the Congress of Europe, held at the Hague in 1948. Under the honorary presidency of Winston Churchill, the

Congress rejected any reconstruction of Europe upon the basis of rigidly divided national sovereignties, called for European unity, and recommended the establishment of the Council. According to Article 3 of the Statute of the Council, every member "must accept the principles of the rule of law and of the enjoyment by all persons within its jurisdiction of human rights and fundamental freedoms. . . ." Article 8 further provides for the suspension of rights of representation for any member that fails to meet its obligations under Article 3.

The competence of the Council is exercised by its Committee of Ministers and Consultative Assembly. In 1949 the Consultative Assembly called upon the Committee of Ministers to establish a collective guarantee for the safeguard of human freedoms. A Committee of Experts was then constituted, and in 1950 the European Convention for the Protection of Human Rights and Fundamental Freedoms was ready for the opinion of the Consultative Assembly; the Assembly approved it on August 25, 1950. it was signed on November 4, 1950, and entered into force on September 3, 1953, upon receipt of the tenth instrument of ratification. The Convention was completed by a Protocol signed on March 20, 1952, which entered into force on May 18, 1954.

The Convention is now binding upon fifteen European states: Austria, Belgium, Cyprus, Denmark, Federal Republic of Germany, Greece, Iceland, Ireland, Italy, Luxembourg, the Netherlands, Norway, Sweden, Turkey, and the United Kingdom. Of these, ten—Austria, Belgium, Denmark, Federal Republic of Germany, Iceland, Ireland, Luxembourg, the Netherlands, Norway, and Sweden—have recognized the competence of the European Commission to receive applications "from any person, nongovernmental organization or group of individuals claiming to be the victim of a violation by one of the High Contracting Parties of the rights set forth" in the Convention. Eight—Austria, Belgium, Denmark, Federal Republic of Germany, Iceland, Ireland, Luxembourg, and the Netherlands—have accepted the compulsory jurisdiction of the supranational European Court of Human Rights. France has not ratified. For a time the principal explanation for this failure was the situation that existed in Algeria, but now that Algeria and the other members of the French community have been granted their independence, it is regrettable that the de Gaulle regime has still taken no action.

The United Kingdom, having ratified the Convention and declared its application to a long list of associated territories, has balked at according the right of individual petition. In this, it is not alone. Cyprus, Greece, Italy, and Turkey also have taken no action aside from ratification. The British government has opposed the full implementation of the Convention:

> They take the view that states are the proper subject of international law and if individuals are given rights under international treaties, effect should be given to those rights through the national law of the states concerned. The reason why we do not accept the idea of compulsory jurisdiction of a European court is because it would mean that British codes of common and statute law would be subject to review by an international court. For many years it has been the position of successive British Governments that we should not accept this status.

The Convention has been criticized with respect to Article 63, which makes discretionary with the member the applicability of the provisions of the instrument to "territories for whose international relations" it is responsible. At present, this article is primarily applicable to the situation of the United Kingdom. In 1953 Her Majesty's Government declared that the European Convention would extend to forty-one territories, from Aden to Zanzibar. Many have since become independent (for example, Malaya, Cyprus, Gold Coast, and Nigeria) or are in the process of achieving control over their international relations. The Netherlands have declared the applicability of the Convention and the Protocol to Surinam and the Netherlands Antilles. Denmark extended the Convention and Protocol to Greenland in 1953, but later in the same year, Greenland became part of metropolitan Denmark, making the extension unnecessary. In similarly worded notes, Belgium and the Netherlands declared that if they do use their discretionary power under Article 63, they will make reservations required by local conditions.

The Protected Rights

A catalog of the fundamental freedoms in the Convention demonstrates a close parallel with our own Bill of Rights with occasional ventures into areas that our Constitution does not consider. Essentially the rights granted in Articles 2 through 12 of the Convention are a compendium of individual civil rights. With few exceptions, neither economic, social, nor cultural rights are included, nor any political rights.

The first four articles secure the right to life and liberty within the protection of the law: no one shall be deprived of his life intentionally except in the execution of a sentence of a court following conviction of a crime for which this penalty is provided by law; torture and other degrading treatment are prohibited; slavery, servitude, and forced or compulsory labor are outlawed. However, service of a military character can be enforced, and the conscientious objector in a country where he is recognized can be made to serve in a nonmilitary capacity. Article 5 ensures freedom from arrest or detention except when imposed in accordance with legal process. It is coupled with the right of what amounts to habeas corpus. Moreover, any victim of an arrest or detention contrary to the provisions of the article has an enforceable right to compensation. The *Lawless* case implemented the Commission's and the Court's power to entertain such proceedings.

Although the Convention contains no general due process clause, the fundamental freedoms necessary to ensure the proper administration of justice are included in Article 6: judgment shall always be pronounced in public although trial may be *in camera* "to the extent strictly necessary in the opinion of the court in special circumstances where publicity would prejudice the interests of justice"; everyone charged with a criminal offense shall be presumed innocent until proved guilty according to law. In all criminal cases the accused must be informed in a language he understands of the charges against him, have adequate time to prepare his defense, be allowed to examine witnesses against him and to obtain the attendance and examination of witnesses on his behalf, and be given the free assistance of an interpreter if he cannot understand or speak the language used in court. The accused has the right to legal assistance, which shall be free if he has insufficient means and the interests of justice so require. At the time of ratification Ireland made a specific reservation to this provision stating that it would not provide any more free legal assistance than was granted before ratification of the Convention. The Netherlands made a specific reservation stating that such legal aid would not be available in Surinam and the Antilles.

Austria declared that the degree of publicity required in court proceedings should be governed by its own constitutional provisions rather than by Article 6.

Article 7 refers to ex post facto criminal punishment: "No one shall be held guilty of any criminal offence on account of any act or omission which did not constitute a criminal offence under national or international law at the time when it was committed." Then, in case the reference to international law was not sufficiently clear, Article 7(2) continues: "This Article shall not prejudice the trial and punishment of any person for any act or omission which, at the time when it was committed, was criminal according to the general principles of law recognized by civilized nations." The Federal Republic of Germany—perhaps with memories of Nuremburg—in its only reservation to the Convention, stipulated that Article 7 of the Convention be applied within the limits of Article 103(2) of the Basic Law of the Federal Republic, providing that an act may be punished only if the law declares it punishable before it has been committed.

The inviolability of every person's private and family life, his home, and his correspondence is ensured. Interference by public authority with the exercise of these rights shall be permitted only so far as necessary in a democratic society. Freedom of religion and worship and freedom of expression—including "freedom to hold opinions and to receive and impart information and ideas without interference by public authority and regardless of frontiers"—is guaranteed. At the time of ratification a reservation was made by Norway to the extent that its constitution outlawed Jesuits. In 1956, however, the reservation was revoked because the Norwegian constitution was amended to eliminate this conflict.

The Convention also grants the right to freedom of assembly and freedom of association, the right to form and join trade unions, and the right to marry. Article 13 requires that anyone whose rights are violated shall have an effective remedy before a national authority even when the violation may have been committed by persons acting officially. Article 14 prohibits discrimination in the enjoyment of the rights and freedoms set forth in the Convention on any ground such as sex, race, color, or political opinion.

In addition to the reservations a state might make to specific provisions, the Convention also contains more general limitations.

. . . Article 15 allows a contracting party in time of war or other public emergency to take measures derogating from its obligations under the Convention. The provisions of Article 2 (right to life), Article 3 (prohibition of torture), Article 4 (prohibition of slavery, and Article 7 (prohibition of ex post facto laws), however, cannot be derogated even under Article 15. In addition, Articles 16 through 18 permit restrictions on the political activity of aliens, that nothing in the Convention may be interpreted as implying the right to engage in any act aimed at the destruction of human rights or freedoms, and limit the restrictions under the Convention to the particular purposes for which they have been prescribed.

In 1952 the parties who ratified the Convention adopted an additional Protocol supplementing the original list of civil rights by certain specific economic and political rights. The Protocol provides that every person is entitled to the peaceful enjoyment of his possessions. It does not prohibit nationalization but is aimed at arbitrary confiscation. . . .

The Protocol further declares that no person shall be denied the right to education, and that the state, in the exercise of any function it assumes in relation to education and teaching, shall respect the rights of parents to ensure that such education and teaching are in conformity with their own religious and philosophical convictions. In addition, the contracting parties undertake to hold free elections at reasonable intervals by secret ballot, under conditions ensuring the free expression of the opinion of the people in the choice of the legislature.

The Protocol, like the body of the Convention itself, is not immediately applicable in affiliated territories of the contracting parties. Moreover, the member states have not generally exercised their discretion to extend the Protocol in this regard; most significantly the United Kingdom has not made it applicable to its territories.

The European Commission of Human Rights

The Convention provides for the creation of two bodies, the Commission and the Court, charged with the responsibility of ensuring "the observance of the engagements undertaken by the High Contracting Parties." The Commission consists of an illustrious group of fourteen jurists and scholars, one from each of the member states of the Council of Europe that have ratified the Convention. Meetings are held at the Council of Europe headquarters in Strasbourg where the "members of the Commission . . . sit on the Commission in their individual capacity."

The Commission was competent to hear applications from one state against another when the Convention came into force in September 1953 but it was not empowered to consider applications from private individuals until July 1955, when the requisite number of member states had recognized the competence of the Commission to hear such petitions. At present, ten states have recognized this competence. The remaining five—Cyprus, Greece, Italy, Turkey, and the United Kingdom—have consequently not been named respondent by any of the individual applications submitted.

The Commission's primary role is to ascertain the facts and to place itself at the disposal of the parties in order to effect a friendly settlement. If no settlement is arranged, the Commission shall draw up a report, which is to be transmitted to the Committee of Ministers, stating whether the facts disclose a breach of the Convention. If the respondent state has not accepted the jurisdiction of the Court of Human Rights, the submission by the Commission to the Committee of Ministers is the ultimate procedural step that can be taken under the terms of the Convention. The Committee must make the final decision unless the case has been referred to the Court within three months from the date of the transmission of the report to the ministers. . . .

The European Court of Human Rights

Article 19(2) of the Convention establishes the European Court of Human Rights whose jurisdiction extends to "all cases concerning the interpretation and application of the present Convention which the High Contracting Parties or the Commission shall refer to it. . . ." Of course this provision applies only to contracting states that have recognized the compulsory jurisdiction of the Court. Moreover, before judges could be elected to the Court, eight declarations accepting such compulsory jurisdiction were required. Five years elapsed before the eight declarations were received; the election of judges was not held until January 21, 1959. Since then the Court has decided two cases. . . .

In any event, besides the foundation it has laid in Europe, the European Convention has already had some profound influence throughout the world. The Federation of Nigeria has included in its constitution a chapter on Human Rights based on the provisions of Section I of the Convention. Similarly, the Republic of Cyprus, now itself an adherent to the Convention, adopted almost to the letter Articles 2-14 of the Convention and Article I of the Protocol in its new constitution. Similar influence is being felt in the Congo, Kenya, Nyasaland, Sierra Leone, Southern Rhodesia, and Uganda. The Law of Lagos, adopted by the African Conference on the Rule of Law, "invites the African Governments to study the possibility of adopting an African Convention of Human Rights in such a manner that the *Conclusions* of the Conference will be safeguarded by the creation of a court of appropriate jurisdiction and that recourse thereto be made available for all persons under the jurisdiction of the signatory states."

Finally, the Organization of American States has undertaken the preliminary tasks of drafting and studying a Convention similar to that created by the Council of Europe for possible adoption in the Western Hemisphere.

One would like to envisage a day when the concept of the European Convention will spread either through adherence to the Convention by additional nations, the formation of similar regional conventions elsewhere in the world, or by endowing the Universal Declaration of Human Rights with powers of enforcement at the petition of individuals. Indeed, Mr. Justice Brennan has suggested the creation of such an international authority. At this stage in history, however, whether the United States would adhere to such a treaty—granting the right of individual petition to challenge decisions of the United States Supreme Court on questions of liberty—can best be indicated by the American refusal to agree to the jurisdiction of the International Court of Justice, reserving to itself the determination whether matters in disputes between states are essentially domestic.

The record of the European Convention is auspicious. One regrets that the Convention is not better known. But the Court decided its first case only in 1960; at a comparable stage, the United States Supreme Court had not given an indication of the role it was ultimately to play in our national development. All analogies are perilous, yet the potential of the European Convention of Human Rights, especially if its operation is more intimately linked with the developing supranational economic institutions in Europe, is at least as great as that of the American Bill of Rights at the commencement of the nineteenth century.

HUMAN RIGHTS FOR MANKIND [5]

Questions of human rights are now at the forefront of international attention. The wall in Berlin, anti-Semitism in the Soviet Union, the general deprivation of human rights in Communist countries, *apartheid* in South Africa, the setbacks for freedom in less developed areas, and the struggle for racial equality in the United States—all have stirred public opinion around the world and profoundly affected international relations.

During most of the first two decades of the United Nations, the drive for freedom tended to be defined as the drive for national independence. But we know that history is studded with examples of unholy alliances between nationalism and tyranny. Now that freedom has been achieved for so many new nations, we are still faced with the previous question: What about freedom for individual men and women and children, the individual human persons whose dignity and worth is reaffirmed on the opening page of the United Nations Charter?

The world today is very far from a satisfactory answer to this question. In some nations, fundamental freedoms are denied by governments as a matter of principle—by racial separation, by political oppression, by religious persecution. In other nations, many freedoms are deliberately postponed, by government action, to concentrate on what are thought to be more urgent items of public business. In all nations in greater or lesser degree, freedoms are threatened by lust for unchallenged political power— by the animosities of tribe or class or caste or sect or party, and by prejudice and bigotry and other evils that still divide the branches of humanity.

[5] From "Human Rights and Foreign Policy," by Richard N. Gardner, Deputy Assistant Secretary of State for International Organization Affairs as published in *Saturday Review.* 47:23-25+. S. 19, '64. This article was a preview of a book by Mr. Gardner, *In Pursuit of World Order: U.S. Foreign Policy and International Organizations.* Frederick A. Praeger, Inc., New York. '64. Reprinted by permission of the latter publisher.

These facts pose a central challenge to United States foreign policy—particularly as prosecuted in international organizations. The United Nations and its affiliated agencies have developed increasingly effective measures to promote two of their great objectives—the maintenance of international peace and security and the promotion of economic and social cooperation. But the members of the United Nations have been not nearly so successful in devising methods to promote the third main objective laid down in the Charter—the promotion of "respect for human rights and for fundamental freedoms for all."

Whether and by what means the United States should seek to rectify this imbalance in the achievements of the United Nations are questions that are urgent, controversial, and complex.

One of the important respects in which the Charter of the United Nations differs from the League of Nations Covenant is in its emphasis on human rights. The Charter makes the promotion of human rights one of the main purposes of the organization. In Articles 55 and 56 the members of the United Nations pledge themselves to take joint and separate action in cooperation with the organization to promote "universal respect for, and observance of, human rights and fundamental freedoms for all without distinction as to race, sex, language or religion." Moreover, Articles 13 and 62 of the Charter charge the General Assembly and the Economic and Social Council [UNESCO] with making recommendations for the advancement of human rights.

These provisions have provided the legal basis for the consideration of human rights questions by the General Assembly and other United Nations organs. It is true that another provision of the Charter, Article 2(7), forbids the United Nations to "intervene in matters which are essentially within the domestic jurisdiction of any state." But when taken together with the human rights provisions of the Charter, this paragraph does not preclude the Assembly and other United Nations organs from carrying on general discussions about the world-wide promotion of human rights that may include specific references to human rights situations in particular countries.

Moreover, the United Nations may consider and adopt recommendations about specific violations of human rights that are part of the member's official policy and inconsistent with its obligations in Articles 55 and 56. This last qualification is important:

it helps explain why United Nations organs have passed recommendations concerning the enforcement of *apartheid* by the government of South Africa and have not passed recommendations about racial discrimination in the United States that is being ardently attacked by the Federal Government. Of course, violations of human rights may be the occasion for mandatory sanctions against a member only when the Security Council determines that they constitute a threat to or breach of international peace.

The Charter of the United Nations also provides for a Commission on Human Rights. Under the chairmanship of Mrs. Eleanor Roosevelt, the Commission undertook as its first major task the drafting of the Universal Declaration of Human Rights, a nonbinding statement of principles to serve as a "common standard of achievement for all peoples and all nations." The Universal Declaration is a comprehensive affirmation of basic political and economic rights found in the Constitution and basic legislation of the United States as well as in the laws of other free countries. [See the text of the Declaration in the next selection.] . . .

Following the adoption of the Universal Declaration, the members of the United Nations turned to the drafting of an international bill of rights in treaty form. In 1951, however, the General Assembly decided to divide the rights enumerated in the Declaration into two legal instruments: a Covenant on Political and Civil Rights embracing the traditional civil and political rights recognized in Western societies, which are generally amenable to legal enforcement; and a Covenant on Economic, Social and Cultural Rights. . . .

Given the difficulties encountered in the negotiation of the comprehensive covenants, it was natural that attention should turn to a more modest approach—the building of an international law of human rights step by step through specific conventions dealing with particular rights.

The Genocide Convention

The first such treaty instrument—the Genocide Convention, which has been in force since 1951—commits the parties to preventing and punishing within their territories the destruction of any national, racial, religious, or ethnic group.

Other United Nations conventions now in force deal with the rights of refugees, stateless persons, the political rights of women, nationality of married women, and slavery.

Also in force are ILO [International Labor Office] conventions on forced labor and discrimination in employment, and a UNESCO Convention on discrimination in education.

In various stages of completion are other UN conventions on racial discrimination, consent to and minimum age of marriage, reduction of statelessness, freedom of information, and the international right to transmit news. [In addition, other agencies of the UN have given attention to human rights problems.]. . .

Problems for United States Policy

The considerations for U.S. leadership in this many-sided UN program in the field of human rights are clear and compelling. They derive in part from the nature of American society. Since the Declaration of Independence the United States has been dedicated to the pursuit of human rights and fundamental freedoms—not just for Americans but for "all men." Throughout American history—and still today—United States power in the world derives not just from its position as an arsenal of weapons or as a storehouse of commodities but as a base from which to seek the universal realization of the dignity of man.

Vigorous American support for human rights around the world is not only an essential and irreversible part of the American tradition; it serves to clarify the issues in the basic struggle for freedom in the world today. Communist leaders put human freedoms very low on their scale of priorities; they are prepared to violate them in their drive for world power and rapid economic growth. The same was true a generation ago of the leaders of the Axis powers. It is the belief in human rights—in the importance and worth of every individual—that distinguishes the United States and other countries of the free world from the totalitarian countries of the left and the right.

We have also learned from hard experience of the intimate interdependence between human rights and peace and security. Nazi Germany should have taught everyone the lesson that internal suppression is often the handmaiden of external aggression—that the destruction of freedom at home can quickly lead to the destruction of freedom abroad. Dictators typically use foreign adventures to solidify their domestic power, and the recklessness of their foreign policy is directly facilitated by the systematic destruction of domestic dissent.

The other side of the coin is no less true: the more a country is threatened from without, the more dangerous it is for human rights within. Those concerned with the preservation and development of human rights in free societies cannot fail to be concerned with the promotion of human rights on a world-wide basis. The same is true for those concerned with the pursuit of peace and security. As President Kennedy asked so eloquently in his American University speech in June of 1963: "Is not peace, in the last analysis, basically, a matter of human rights . . . ?" World-wide progress in the vindication of human rights and fundamental freedoms will also be progress toward creating a peaceful and stable world order.

Of course, the international promotion of human rights is not a one-way street. World opinion is concerned not only with human rights problems of other countries but also with human rights problems in the United States—particularly with the struggle for racial equality. Some Americans fear that an attempt to assert United States leadership in the international promotion of human rights may result in unwanted international attention to our domestic problems. They raise the question: As the price for putting the heat on others, are we prepared to take the heat ourselves?

To a large extent, this question has already been answered for us. The United States is an open society with the world's most highly developed media of mass communication. Our domestic racial problems are widely advertised to every corner of the globe. So we are already "taking the heat" of intense international attention.

The same is not true for the closed societies of the world. In these countries—where the press is controlled and foreign newsmen are severely restricted in their freedom of movement—violations of human rights do not automatically succeed in impressing themselves on world opinion. Thus, there tends to be a geographic imbalance in the focus of international attention to human rights problems.

Nor is the imbalance one of geography alone. The current international preoccupation in the field of human rights is on racial discrimination and specifically on the struggle for Negro equality. The vindication of the rights of Negro communities in the United States and elsewhere is a matter of urgent public business. But there are other human rights questions besides the question of Negro equality. In the preoccupation with how white men treat black men the world must not lose sight of how white men treat white men, or how black men treat black men, or even how black men come to terms with the white minorities in their midst.

Human rights, like the United States Constitution, should be color-blind in every sense of the phrase. In a world becoming increasingly race-conscious, there is a particular danger that violations of human rights within racial groups will tend to be ignored. The problem was poignantly illustrated in a recent cartoon that shows a smiling Mao Tse-tung telling an African leader: "Of course, there is no discrimination in China. Here we enslave everybody!"

The choices facing the United States in the field of human rights are therefore clear. On the one hand, it can take a defensive posture out of concern with its domestic difficulties. In this event, the world's concern with the racial issue in the United States will not go away. On the contrary, the present disparity between the world's attention to racial discrimination—as manifested particularly in the United States—and other kinds of human rights violations in other countries will probably increase.

On the other hand, the United States can assert its leadership in the world-wide promotion of human rights. In this case, it can broaden international awareness and concern with human rights problems into an objective examination of the state of human dignity in all countries and thus place the struggle for equality in the United States in its total world setting.

The United States is already in the sun. Any additional light on human rights that can be generated through the United Nations will do more to illumine the deprivations of these rights in the dark corners of closed societies than in the open societies of the free world.

Recent experience suggests that the long-term interests of our country may well be served by fuller information on our struggle

for racial equality. Criticisms of U.S. racial problems in the UN
by the Soviet Union and others have attracted little support in
recent years—partly because UN members have been increasingly
impressed by the efforts of the Federal Government to assure
civil rights for all our citizens.

UN delegates who have traveled widely in the United States
frequently become our best defenders. A case in point is the visit
to Atlanta arranged in January 1964 for members of the Subcommission on Discrimination and Minorities. The members of
the Subcommission were invited wholly in their personal capacities as individuals known to be interested in the city's progress.
Nevertheless, fears were immediately expressed that they would
concentrate on adverse aspects of race problms with a view to dis-
crediting the United States in the UN. Further objections were
voiced when it was found that the visit would coincide with re-
newed demonstrations by local student organizations against
restaurants that had not yet desegregated.

All these fears proved groundless. The visitors toured all sections of Atlanta and talked freely with citizen and protest groups
as well as city officials and the press. All were favorably impressed, not only with the city's determination to achieve racial
equality but, even more, with the concern of the police for free
speech and a fair hearing for all involved in controversy, whatever their views might be.

There are many different ways, of course, of promoting human
rights. The United States has a powerful lever in its bilateral
diplomacy. Increasing opportunities for action on human rights
questions are becoming available in regional forums. In some
cases, quiet representations to a government or an informal and
ad hoc process of conciliation may produce the best results. But
the experience of recent years also suggests the utility of exposing
human rights problems to world attention in the global forums
of the United Nations where they can be looked at by the community of nations as a whole.

The American interest in promoting the human rights activities of the United Nations has already been expressed through
vigorous leadership in a number of areas. The United States
played the leading role through the person of Mrs. Roosevelt, in
the preparation of the Universal Declaration of Human Rights.
It sponsored the "action" program to strengthen human rights

through national reporting, research, and advisory services. It has left no doubt about its position when violations of human rights from South Africa to Tibet have been brought before United Nations forums.

Yet the United States is now being challenged to take further leadership in United Nations activity in human rights. The Administration has reaffirmed support for ratification of the Genocide Convention. And, in July of 1963, President Kennedy submitted to the Senate for advice and consent to ratification the conventions dealing with slavery, forced labor, and the political rights of women. Although the legal standards established by these conventions are already reflected in our Constitution and statutes, and have long been deeply rooted in our legal and moral heritage, the United States has so far not ratified them, or any other human rights convention drafted under UN auspices—a fact that many find hard to understand.

Obviously, words on paper are not enough. Nobody believes that the signing of a human rights convention in and of itself brings automatic improvement in the condition of people around the world. But United States participation in the great effort, under United Nations auspices, to define and clarify basic human rights can make a practical contribution to the national interest in promoting human rights in at least three ways:

First, United States ratification can stimulate other nations to adhere to these conventions and can augment their impact among countries already parties to them. The United States will thus be encouraging the implementation of these basic human rights standards within foreign countries.

Second, ratification will put the United States in a better legal and moral position to protest infringement of these human rights in countries that have ratified the conventions but failed to implement them in practice.

Third, ratification will increase United States influence in the continuing United Nations process of the drafting of legal norms in the field of human rights. So long as the United States fails to ratify any human rights conventions, its views will carry less weight than they deserve.

Beyond ratification of human rights treaties, more can be done with the existing resources of the United Nations—particularly through the opportunities for influencing international opinion in the General Assembly and the Human Rights Commission. The potentiality of the United Nations in this connection has been graphically illustrated on many occasions—most recently when the United States brought the issue of anti-Semitism in the Soviet Union to the attention of the Human Rights Commission . . . [in March 1964].

Existing UN procedures, however, may not be sufficient. In the words of Harlan Cleveland [Assistant Secretary of State for International Organization Affairs]:

The problem we need to consider is how sharp beams of international light can be effectively poked into the world's darkest recesses of reaction—and how those beams once inside can be focused and intensified until, like the laser ray, they burn out the malignancy of man's inhumanity to man.

At the present time the beams of international light are not sharp and fully focused. The only comprehensive information received by the Commission on Human Rights is a survey every three years, based on reports submitted by member governments. These reports are generally bland and incomplete; many countries fail to report at all. Moreover, the incoming material is not made available in original form; the document prepared for the Commission is merely a summary of what has been received, so that governments are spared direct exposure of self-serving omissions and interpretations. The *Human Rights Yearbook*, published regularly three years after date, consists only of legislation, court decisions, and official documents. Discussion in the Human Rights Commission is further inhibited by the tradition that reference should not be made to a specific situation or a specific country.

The result of all this is that the Human Rights Commission regularly bypasses discussions of current problems in specific countries. In the vacuum thus created, the General Assembly has tended to involve itself in political and emotional discussions of a few human rights problems without the benefit of a broad and analytical review of the entire subject. And the United Nations as a whole lacks an up-to-date, comprehensive, and professional analysis of the measures taken by member states in fulfillment of their obligations to promote human rights for all their citizens.

In the months ahead, the U.S. and other UN members will be considering possible ways to strengthen the work of the United Nations in the field of human rights—in defining standards, in clarifying experience, in reviewing government performance against Charter principles, and in exposing to the conscience of the world the denial of those rights that should be the heritage of all human beings.

Thus new opportunities may be available in the international promotion of human rights—particularly through a process of publicity and persuasion. But such a process can work successfully only if the nations participating in it are genuinely devoted to the national pursuit of human rights—not the national pursuit of self-righteousness. In this field we might well benefit from the application of the familiar legal doctrine of "clean hands"; those who would call in question the practices of others should at least be making every effort to put their own house in order. For the real test of a nation's commitment to human rights is not what it says in the United Nations for all the world to hear, but what it does at home for all the world to see. As Mrs. Roosevelt put it some years ago: "It is not just a question of getting the [Human Rights] Covenants written and accepted . . . it is a question of actually living and working in our countries for freedom and justice for each human being."

THE UNIVERSAL DECLARATION OF HUMAN RIGHTS [6]

Preamble

WHEREAS recognition of the inherent dignity and of the equal and inalienable rights of all members of the human family is the foundation of freedom, justice and peace in the world,

WHEREAS disregard and contempt for human rights have resulted in barbarous acts which have outraged the conscience of mankind, and the advent of a world in which human beings shall enjoy freedom of speech and belief and freedom from fear and want has been proclaimed as the highest aspiration of the common people,

WHEREAS it is essential, if man is not to be compelled to have recourse, as a last resort, to rebellion against tyranny and oppression, that human rights should be protected by the rule of law,

[6] Reprinted from *UNESCO Courier.* 16:16-17. D. '63.

WHEREAS it is essential to promote the development of friendly relations between nations,

WHEREAS the peoples of the United Nations have in the Charter reaffirmed their faith in fundamental human rights, in the dignity and worth of the human person and in the equal rights of men and women and have determined to promote social progress and better standards of life in larger freedom,

WHEREAS member states have pledged themselves to achieve, in cooperation with the United Nations, the promotion of universal respect for and observance of human rights and fundamental freedoms,

WHEREAS a common understanding of these rights and freedoms is of the greatest importance for the full realization of this pledge,

NOW THEREFORE THE GENERAL ASSEMBLY PROCLAIMS THIS UNIVERSAL DECLARATION OF HUMAN RIGHTS as a common standard of achievement for all peoples and all nations, to the end that every individual and every organ of society, keeping the Declaration constantly in mind, shall strive by teaching and education to promote respect for these rights and freedoms and by progressive measures, national and international, to secure their universal and effective recognition and observance, both among the peoples of member states themselves and among the peoples of territories under their jurisdiction.

Article 1

All human beings are born free and equal in dignity and rights. They are endowed with reason and conscience and should act towards one another in a spirit of brotherhood.

Article 2

Everyone is entitled to all the rights and freedoms set forth in this Declaration, without distinction of any kind, such as race, color, sex, language, religion, political or other opinion, national or social origin, property, birth or other status.

Furthermore, no distinction shall be made on the basis of the political, jurisdictional or international status of the country or territory to which a person belongs, whether it be independent, trust, non-self-governing or under any other limitation of sovereignty.

Article 3

Everyone has the right to life, liberty and security of person.

Article 4

No one shall be held in slavery or servitude; slavery and the slave trade shall be prohibited in all their forms.

Article 5

No one shall be subjected to torture or to cruel, inhuman or degrading treatment or punishment.

Article 6

Everyone has the right to recognition everywhere as a person before the law.

Article 7

All are equal before the law and are entitled without any discrimination to equal protection of the law. All are entitled to equal protection against any discrimination in violation of this Declaration and against any incitement to such discrimination.

Article 8

Everyone has the right to an effective remedy by the competent national tribunals for acts violating the fundamental rights granted him by the constitution or by law.

Article 9

No one shall be subjected to arbitrary arrest, detention or exile.

Article 10

Everyone is entitled in full equality to a fair and public hearing by an independent and impartial tribunal, in the determination of his rights and obligations and of any criminal charge against him.

Article 11

(1) Everyone charged with a penal offense has the right to be presumed innocent until proved guilty according to law in a public trial at which he has had all the guarantees necessary for his defense.

(2) No one shall be held guilty of any penal offense on account of any act or omission which did not constitute a penal offense, under national or international law, at the time when it was committed. Nor shall a heavier penalty be imposed than the one that was applicable at the time the penal offense was committed.

Article 12

No one shall be subjected to arbitrary interference with his privacy, family, home or correspondence, nor to attacks upon his honor and reputation. Everyone has the right to the protection of the law against such interference or attacks.

Article 13

(1) Everyone has the right to freedom of movement and residence within the borders of each state.

(2) Everyone has the right to leave any country, including his own, and to return to his country.

Article 14

(1) Everyone has the right to seek and to enjoy in other countries asylum from persecution.

(2) This right may not be invoked in the case of prosecutions genuinely arising from nonpolitical crimes or from acts contrary to the purposes and principles of the United Nations.

Article 15

(1) Everyone has the right to a nationality.

(2) No one shall be arbitrarily deprived of his nationality nor denied the right to change his nationality.

Article 16

(1) Men and women of full age, without any limitation due to race, nationality or religion, have the right to marry and to found a family. They are entitled to equal rights as to marriage, during marriage and at its dissolution.

(2) Marriage shall be entered into only with the free and full consent of the intending spouses.

(3) The family is the natural and fundamental group unit of society and is entitled to protection by society and the state.

Article 17

(1) Everyone has the right to own property alone as well as in association with others.

(2) No one shall be arbitrarily deprived of his property.

Article 18

Everyone has the right to freedom of thought, conscience and religion; this right includes freedom to change his religion or belief, and freedom, either alone or in community with others and in public or private, to manifest his religion or belief in teaching, practice. worship and observance.

Article 19

Everyone has the right to freedom of opinion and expression; this right includes freedom to hold opinions without interference and to seek, receive and impart information and ideas through any media and regardless of frontiers.

Article 20

(1) Everyone has the right to freedom of peaceful assembly and association.

(2) No one may be compelled to belong to an association.

Article 21

(1) Everyone has the right to take part in the government of his country, directly or through freely chosen representatives.

(2) Everyone has the right of equal access to public service in his country.

(3) The will of the people shall be the basis of the authority of government; this will shall be expressed in periodic and genuine elections which shall be by universal and equal suffrage and shall be held by secret vote or by equivalent free voting procedures.

Article 22

Everyone, as a member of society, has the right to social security and is entitled to realization, through national effort and international cooperation and in accordance with the organization and resources of each state, of the economic, social and cultural rights indispensable for his dignity and the free development of his personality.

Article 23

(1) Everyone has the right to work, to free choice of employment, to just and favorable conditions of work and to protection against unemployment.

(2) Everyone, without any discrimination, has the right to equal pay for equal work.

(3) Everyone who works has the right to just and favorable remuneration ensuring for himself and his family an existence worthy of human dignity, and supplemented, if necessary, by other means of social protection.

(4) Everyone has the right to form and to join trade unions for the protection of his interests.

Article 24

Everyone has the right to rest and leisure, including reasonable limitation of working hours and periodic holidays with pay.

Article 25

(1) Everyone has the right to a standard of living adequate for the health and well-being of himself and of his family, including food, clothing, housing and medical care and necessary social services, and the right to security in the event of unemployment, sickness, disability, widowhood, old age or other lack of livelihood in circumstances beyond his control.

(2) Motherhood and childhood are entitled to special care and assistance. All children, whether born in or out of wedlock, shall enjoy the same social protection.

Article 26

(1) Everyone has the right to education. Education shall be free, at least in the elementary and fundamental stages. Elementary education shall be compulsory. Technical and professional education shall be made generally available and higher education shall be equally accessible to all on the basis of merit.

(2) Education shall be directed to the full development of the human personality and to the strengthening of respect for human rights and fundamental freedoms. It shall promote understanding, tolerance and friendship among all nations, racial or religious groups, and shall further the activities of the United Nations for the maintenance of peace.

(3) Parents have a prior right to choose the kind of education that shall be given to their children.

Article 27

(1) Everyone has the right freely to participate in the cultural life of the community, to enjoy the arts and to share in scientific advancement and its benefits.

(2) Everyone has the right to the protection of the moral and material interests resulting from any scientific, literary or artistic production of which he is the author.

Article 28

Everyone is entitled to a social and international order in which the rights and freedoms set forth in this Declaration can be fully realized.

Article 29

(1) Everyone has duties to the community in which alone the free and full development of his personality is possible.

(2) In the exercise of his rights and freedoms, everyone shall be subject only to such limitations as are determined by law solely for the purpose of securing due recognition and respect for the rights and freedoms of others and of meeting the just requirements of morality, public order and the general welfare in a democratic society.

(3) These rights and freedoms may in no case be exercised contrary to the purposes and principles of the United Nations.

Article 30

Nothing in this Declaration may be interpreted as implying for any state, group or person any right to engage in any activity or to perform any act aimed at the destruction of any of the rights and freedoms set forth herein.

BIBLIOGRAPHY

An asterisk (*) preceding a reference indicates that the article or a part of it has been reprinted in this book.

BOOKS, PAMPHLETS, AND DOCUMENTS

Ahmann, M. H. ed. New Negro. Fides. Notre Dame, Ind. '61.

Baldwin, James. Fire next time. Dial Press. New York. '63.

Booker, Simeon. Black man's America. Prentice-Hall. Englewood Cliffs, N.J. '64.

Brink, William and Harris, Louis. Negro revolution in America. Simon and Schuster. New York. '64.

Brooks, A. D. comp. Civil rights and liberties in the United States: an annotated bibliography. Civil Liberties Educational Foundation. 200 Park Ave. S. New York, N.Y. 10003. '62.

Cahn, Edmond, ed. Great rights. Macmillan. New York. '63.

Carr, R. K. Federal protection of civil rights. Cornell University Press. Ithaca, N.Y. '64.

Chafee, Zechariah, Jr. Blessings of liberty. Lippincott. Philadelphia. '56.

Cranston, M. W. What are human rights? Basic Books. New York. '63.

Daniel, Bradford, ed. Black, white, and gray. Sheed and Ward. New York. '64.

Douglas, W. O. Democracy's manifesto. Doubleday. Garden City, N.Y. '62.

Douglas, W. O. Freedom of the mind. Public Affairs Committee. 22 E. 38th St. New York, N.Y. 10016. '62.

Fraenkel, O. K. The Supreme Court and civil liberties. Oceana. Dobbs Ferry, N.Y. '63.

*Gardner, R. N. In pursuit of world order: U.S. foreign policy and international organizations. Frederick A. Praeger. New York. '64.
  Reprinted in this book: Preview of book with title, Human rights and foreign policy. Saturday Review. 47:23-5+. S. 19, '64.

Greenberg, Jack. Race relations and American law. Columbia University Press. New York. '59.

Hand, Learned. Bill of Rights. Atheneum. New York. '64.

Handlin, Oscar. Fire-bell in the night. Little, Brown. Boston. '64.

Hentoff, Nat. New equality. Viking. New York. '64.

Hughes, Langston. Fight for freedom: the story of the NAACP. Norton. New York. '62.

Human Rights. Oceana. Dobbs Ferry, N.Y. '63.

Isaacs, H. R. New world of Negro Americans. John Day. New York. '63.

Johnson, L. B. and others. Negro as an American. Center for the Study of Democratic Institutions. Box 4068. Santa Barbara, Calif. '63.

Kahn, Tom. Economics of equality. League for Industrial Democracy. New York. '64.

Kauper, P. G. Civil liberties and the Constitution. University of Michigan Press. Ann Arbor. '62.

Kennedy, R. F. Rights for Americans. Bobbs-Merrill. Indianapolis. '64.

King, M. L. Jr. Letter from Birmingham city jail. American Friends Service Committee. Philadelphia. '63.

*King, M. L. Jr. Why we can't wait. Harper. New York. '64.
    Adaptation of Chapter 8. Life 56:98-100+. My. 15, '64.

Konvitz, M. R. ed. Bill of Rights reader. Cornell University Press. Ithaca, N.Y. '64.

Konvitz, M. R. and Leskes, Theodore. Century of civil rights. Columbia University Press. New York. '61.

La Farge, John. Catholic viewpoint on race relations. Doubleday. Garden City. N.Y. '60.

Lewis, Anthony. Gideon's trumpet. Random House. New York. '64.

Lewis, Anthony, ed. Portrait of a decade. Random House. New York. '64.

Lincoln, C. E. Black Muslims in America. Beacon Press. Boston. '61.

Lomax, L. E. Negro revolt. Harper. New York. '62.

Lomax, L. E. When the word is given. World. Cleveland. '63.

Lubell, Samuel. White and black: test of a nation. Harper. New York. '64.

Malin, P. M. "Testing whether that nation"; 41st annual report of the American Civil Liberties Union. The Union. 156 Fifth Ave. New York. '61.

Marshall, Burke. Federalism and civil rights. Columbia University Press. New York. '64.

Myrdal, Gunnar. American dilemma. Harper. New York. '62.

*National Urban League. "Marshall Plan" for the American Negro; statement of the League, June 9, 1963. The League. 14 E. 48th St. New York, N.Y. 10017. '63.

Newman, E. S., ed. Freedom reader. Oceana. Dobbs Ferry, N.Y. '63.

*Passow, A. H. ed. Education in depressed areas. Teachers College, Columbia University. New York. '63.
    Reprinted in this book: Educational problems of segregation and desegregation. J. H. Fischer. p 291-6.

Patterson, Barbara, et al. Price we pay. Anti-Defamation League. 515 Madison Ave. New York, N.Y. 10022. '64.

Schwelb, Egon. Human rights and the international community. Quadrangle. Chicago. '64.

Silberman, C. E. Crisis in black and white. Random House. New York. '64.
    Excerpt with title: Businessman and the Negro. Fortune. 68:97-9+. S. '63.

Toward civil rights now. The Progressive. Madison, Wis. '64.
    Reprints from 1963 and 1964 issues of The Progressive.

United States. Commission on Civil Rights. Civil rights '63. report of the Commission. Supt. of Docs. Washington, D.C. 20025. '63.

*United States. Congress. Senate. Committee on the Judiciary. Sub-
committee on Constitutional Rights. Layman's guide to individual
rights under the United States Constitution. 87th Congress. 2d
session. Supt. of Docs. Washington, D.C. 20025. '62.

Welsch, E. K., comp. Negro in the United States; a research guide. Indiana University Library. Bloomington. '64.

Westin, A. F. Freedom now! Basic Books. New York. '64.

Young, W. M., Jr. To be equal. McGraw-Hill. New York. '64.

Periodicals

American Bar Association Journal. 50:151. F. '64. Civil rights and civil
wrongs. E. F. Cummerford.
      Same: U.S. News & World Report. 56:84-6. F. 17, '64.

*American Bar Association Journal. 50:540-4. Je. '64. Electronic eaves-
dropping: trespass by device. J. T. Lynch.

*American Political Science Review. 57:841-54. D. '63. Rights, liber-
ties, freedoms—a reappraisal. C. J. Friedrich.

Atlantic. 211:42-6. Ja. '63. White liberal's retreat. Murray Friedman.

Christian Century. 80:168-71. F. 6, '63. 'New Negro' and the Protestant
churches. G. S. Wilmore, Jr.

*Columbia Law Review. 63:1384-1412. D. '63. New horizons for hu-
man rights: the European convention, court, and commission of
human rights. Jack Greenberg and A. R. Shalit.

Columbia Law Review. 64:193-229. F. '64. Decade of school desegregation. A. M. Bickel.

Commentary. 35:10-14. Ja. '63. Housing order and its limits. Charles
Abrams.

Commentary. 35:93-101. F. '63. My Negro problem—and ours. Nor-
man Podhoretz.

*Commentary. 38:33-9. Ag. '64. Civil Rights Act of 1964. A. M.
Bickel.

Dissent. 11:108-38. Winter '64. Problems of the Negro movement.
Tom Kahn.

Ebony. 18:66-71. S. '63. Role of the middle-class Negro. W. M.
Young, Jr.

*Ebony. 18:99-100+. S. '63. South looks ahead. Ralph McGill.

*Ebony. 18:221-2+. S. '63. Constitution—key to freedom. C. B. Motley.

Editorial Research Reports. 1:87-104. F. 6. '63. Interracial housing.
H. B. Shaffer.

Fellowship. 30:5-8. Jl. '64. Nonviolence on trial. Bayard Rustin.

*Harper's Magazine. 288:69-70+. Mr. '64. Justice with a Southern
accent. Louis Lusky.

Journal of Politics. 26:1-240. F. '64. American South: 1950-1970. Avery Leiserson, ed.

*Law and Contemporary Problems. 28:447-86. Summer '63. Academic freedom—an emerging constitutional right. W. P. Murphy.

Liberation. 9:21-6. Ag. '64. Cybernation and human rights. Robert Theobald.

Nation. 197:25-8. Jl. 13, '63. Religious freedom. T. G. Sanders.

*Nation. 198:367-72. Ap. 13, '64. Justice for the poor; the banner of Gideon. R. G. Sherrill.

Nation. 199:243-6. O. 19, '64. Welfare or status. E. C. Ladd, Jr.

*National Observer. p 13. Je. 22, '64. What the new rights measure provides.

New Republic. 151:15-16. Ag. 22, '64. Crime, wealth and justice. Ronald Goldfarb.

*New Republic. 151:17-21. Ag. 22, '64. Mississippi; from conversion to coercion. Christopher Jencks.

New South. 19:1-28. Ja. '64. The Southern Regional Council 1944-1964.

New South. 19:29-32. Ja. '64. Statement of views. Executive Committee of the Southern Regional Council.

New York Times. p 36. Je. 24, '62. Global civil rights.

*New York Times. p 20. Je. 12, '63. Television address on civil rights, June 11, 1963. J. F. Kennedy.

New York Times. p 36. Mr. 10, '64. Free press and free people.

New York Times. p 20. Mr. 11, '64. Libel and the Constitution. Anthony Lewis.

*New York Times. p 10E. Mr. 15, '64. Court broadens freedom of the press. Anthony Lewis.

*New York Times. p 18. Je. 19, '64. Speech to United States Senate on civil rights, Je. 18, '64. Barry Goldwater.

*New York Times. p 32. Je. 23, '64. Subversion in travel.

*New York Times. p 9. Jl. 3, '64. Address on civil rights, Jl. 2, '64. L. B. Johnson.

New York Times Magazine. p 7+. Je. 17, '62. Historic change in the Supreme Court. Anthony Lewis.

New York Times Magazine. p 26-7+. My. 12, '63. Two ways: Black Muslim and NAACP. Gertrude Samuels.

New York Times Magazine. p 43+. O. 6, '63. Should there be 'compensation' for Negroes? Two views. W. M. Young, Jr.; Kyle Haselden.

New York Times Magazine. p 17+. Ja. 12, '64. Is it ever right to break the law? Charles Frankel.

*New York Times Magazine. p 14+. F. 9, '64. Negro's problem is the white's. Eli Ginzberg.

New York Times Magazine. p 24+. Mr. 15, '64. Equal justice for the poor, too. A. J. Goldberg.

*New York Times Magazine. p 9+. My. 10, '64. Since the Supreme Court spoke. Anthony Lewis.

*New York Times Magazine. p 14+. My. 17, '64. Five angry men speak their minds. Gertrude Samuels.

New York Times Magazine. p 11+. My. 31, '64. Plea for a 'new phase in Negro leadership.' Daniel Bell.

*New York Times Magazine p 7+. Ag. 9, '64. Much more than law is needed. A. M. Bickel.

New York Times Magazine. p 11+. Ag. 16, '64. What now?—one Negro leader's answer. Roy Wilkins.

New York Times Magazine. p 27+. Ag. 23, '64. Analysis of the 'white-backlash.' W. L. Miller.

New York Times Magazine. p 23+. S. 20, '64. Walls do have ears. Vance Packard.

New York Times Magazine. p 30+. N. 22, '64. Race, Sex and the Supreme Court. Anthony Lewis.

Progressive. D. '62. Century of struggle: Emancipation Proclamation, 1863-1963. Special issue.

Reporter. 31:44-6. Ag. 13, '64. South learns to live with the civil-rights law. Pat Watters.

Saturday Review. 47:23-5+. S. 19, '64. Human rights and foreign policy. R. N. Gardner.

*UNESCO Courier. 16:16-17. D. '63. Text of the Universal Declaration of Human Rights.

U.S. News & World Report. 54:46-52. Ap. 29, '63. What the American Negro wants; interview with Roy Wilkins.

U.S. News & World Report. 56:99-101. Mr. 23, '64. Can "integration" be forced by Federal law? C. E. Whittaker.

*Vital Speeches of the Day. 28:706-8. S. 15, '62. Judicial administration. R. F. Kennedy.

Vital Speeches of the Day. 29:30-2. O. 15, '62. Rights of children. R. F. Drinan.

*Vital Speeches of the Day. 29:220-2. Ja. 15, '63. Freedom of speech. LeRoy Collins.

*Vital Speeches of the Day. 30:61-4. N. 1, '63. Food, jobs and human rights. Robert Theobald.

Vital Speeches of the Day. 30:535-7. Je. 15, '64. Civil rights: discrimination in labor unions. W. M. Young, Jr.

*Washington Post. p E1+. Je. 28, '64. 1954-64 truly an era. J. E. Clayton.

23409